Coton de Tule:

or Coton.

Coton de Tulear Complete Dog Manual

Coton de Tulear dog care, costs, feeding, grooming, health and training all included.

by

Matthew Burston

*Dog Lover and Dog Owner*

# Disclaimer

Published by IMB Publishing

# Table of Contents

# Table of Contents

# Table of Contents

## Table of Contents

7

# Foreword

There are over 150 distinctive dog breeds in the world. Each breed possesses unique characteristics. This makes every dog breed lovable for its individuality!

But there is one thing that remains more or less consistent across all breeds – they make fine companions. Most dogs are extremely loyal to their owners.

If trained well, they have the tendency to mirror their owner's wishes even before they express it verbally. Their association comes bundled with wonderful memories, cuddlesome experiences and some finest moments that remain embedded in the mind forever!

Here you will find detailed information about the Coton de Tulear breed – how to take care of it and feed it, how to go about its grooming and training concerns, and everything pertaining to this outclass breed.

Everything you need to know about the Coton de Tulear dog breed is contained in this guide. Read through carefully before you decide to bring your canine companion home.

# Chapter 1: Introduction

There are over 150 dog breeds that are classified under different categories like the large breeds, the small breeds, the working group, the toy group, the sporting group, the non-sporting group, the herding group and so on and so forth. The characteristics of dogs under each category are more or less quite similar.

The Coton de Tulear dog breed is regarded as a small breed companion dog owing to its amiable nature and cuddlesome appearance. The breed acquired its name from the word "Cotton" which implies its soft hairy coat.

The Coton de Tulear dog is a humble representation of beauty, intelligence, loyalty, companionship and playfulness. It is a "little cotton ball" which keeps you happily entertained throughout the relationship.

Besides this, its small size makes it a compact, manageable and "mobile" pet. Many of the problems associated with transporting large breeds are absent, so it becomes easier to care for the Coton de Tulear dog.

This also means the dog will not be occupying a significant chunk of your house space. Instead, it will fit into almost any corner!

And when it comes to pulling off those amazing god-gifted looks, this particular breed has a knack of flaunting its beauty in breath-taking style! This makes the dog even more adorable!

But before you start thinking about getting a Coton de Tulear dog, there are a lot of things you need to consider and evaluate against each other. Carefully assessed decisions are less likely to end up in failure compared to gut-instinct purchases!

For instance, take some time to ask yourself; do you really want a Coton de Tulear dog or are you possibly looking for a guardian dog? Are there other dog breeds that you find more exciting than the Coton de Tulear? Know what you really want before you actually go through the trouble of purchasing one!

And if you are worried about how, where, and for how much to buy a Coton de Tulear, this book will have the right answers for you! In addition to this, we have also included detailed information about how to care for this breed for a truly wonderful journey up ahead.

Everything you need to know about this breed is contained here. Keep reading to find out if Coton de Tulear is really the dog you are looking for. And once you've made the decision to buy, get one immediately!

# Chapter 2: Coton de Tulear – The Cotton Ball

Has it ever happened with you that you saw someone carrying an oddly shaped baggy cushion in their arms and you had to double back to notice that it actually had eyes, a nose and a mouth hidden beneath layers of soft hair?

Or what you thought to be a misplaced cushion in the drawing room suddenly moved on its own so you actually had to look really closely to see it wasn't really a cushion?

There are a couple of animals that are blessed with auspicious amounts of hair that not only cover their entire body but also their face. So to the uninformed observer, they merely appear to be a soft ball.

The Coton de Tulear dog is one such animal that has been blessed with copious amounts of soft hair which gives it the look of a cushion. And when it is curled up like one, it would surely be difficult to differentiate!

This particular dog breed has enjoyed its fair share of attention. Who wouldn't turn to look at a small and fluffy white cotton ball walking proudly on the red carpet in a dog show? And with the style and grace of someone absolutely sure of itself! The Coton de Tulear is definitely a sight to see!

This book is dedicated to the likeness of this wonderful dog – its characteristics, features, temperament, lifestyle, grooming needs, feeding needs and everything else that is important for a seamless transition into companionship!

So if you are looking forward to buying a Coton de Tulear dog or are simply wondering if it is really the dog for you, keep reading and put all your curiosities at peace.

11

In any case, how much could a small fragile dog like the Coton de Tulear really hurt?

## 1) *Some Facts about the Coton de Tulear Breed*

The Coton de Tulear breed is quite popular amidst a wide proportion of dog enthusiasts. It has reached new heights in terms of recognition over the past two decades!

Here are some interesting facts about the Coton de Tulear breed that makes it a truly amazing dog breed to pet.

1. The Coton de Tulear was quite popular with the nobles of Tulear in Madagascar. In fact, it became a symbol of luxury and sophistication for the residents of Madagascar.

2. The Coton is believed to be a mixed breed. Experts say that the national dog of Madagascar was bred with a foreign dog coming in from France with French troops. The result was unexpectedly beautiful!
In essence, the Coton de Tulear breed did not exist from the beginning but was created somewhere within the last century.

3. The Coton breed has existed for at least a century and has enjoyed a rather privileged status in Madagascar. Despite this, the official worldwide recognition for this breed is merely two decades!

4. Cross breeding can cause inherent mutations which may emerge as genetic health problems later on. The Coton de Tulear is one of those cases in which genetic mutation actually helped overcome genetic problems faced by earlier breeds.

5. The Coton de Tulear is extremely hairy and may seem like a ferocious hair shedder. However, contrary to this expectation, this breed is known to shed little to no hair!
It may come as a surprise for most people. This is also the reason

why it makes a perfect canine companion for people with allergies.

6. Despite its apparently small size and therefore a small energy reserve and stamina, the Coton de Tulear dog can follow its horse mounted owner for several miles at a stretch. For a dog of its size and personality, this is a shockingly colossal achievement!

7. The Coton de Tulear likes to keep its owners happy and may go an extra mile just to do so. It may jump up and walk on its hind legs just to see the owner laugh.
This characteristic is embedded in its genetic code.

8. The Coton is a small breed that is adorned with natural beauty. Consequently, a lot of its "offensive" activities do not look the same.
In fact, it may look outright endearing to see a Coton de Tulear jump into the owner's lap. This, however, leads to personality issues and may cause behavioral problems later on.

9. The Coton de Tulear was originally given the name "Royal dog of Madagascar" for its in-built majesty. It was later rephrased to "Coton de Tulear" with literally means the "Cotton of Tulear"

10. The Coton breed is largely an indoor dog breed that enjoys the company of its owners. However, taking it out for a walk in the park or a swim across a lake can actually make it happy beyond expression.
And it is really endearing to see the small ball running around different objects, jumping up and cheering in the foreign environment!

There is a lot to the Coton de Tulear than what meets the eye. The soft and innocent eyes hold great secrets. Most of these will be detailed through this book.

It is now time to discuss its known history in brief to give you an idea of where the beauty and brains came from. So here goes!

## 2) *A Brief History of Coton de Tulear*

As mentioned previously, the history of the Coton de Tulear breed is a little complicated. In fact, certain records contain contradictory information about the emergence of this breed!

Here is the popular idea revolving around the evolution of the Coton de Tulear breed.

The history of Coton de Tulear's early ancestors can be traced back to the $16^{th}$ and $17^{th}$ centuries when Madagascar was particularly popular for pirate invasions.

The pirate ships docked at Madagascar quite often. There are quite a few pirate graveyards in this part of the world to substantiate the presence of pirates on the land.

It is not clear if the dogs brought on the land by the pirates were their companions or merely spoils of war taken from destroyed ships.

Nevertheless, the first Coton de Tulear ancestors entered into the land and hence began the Coton de Tulear legacy.

The alternative theory to this, however, states that the first ancestors for this breed came along with French troops and administrators during the $19^{th}$ century. The French invasion of Madagascar is not news. So this anecdote seems to be a more likely truth.

The "foreign" dogs that were brought into the land (either from pirate invasion or from the French invasion) bred with the local dogs of the island.

The result was Coton de Tulear! This is how the breed was born!

Then on, however, pure breeding was practiced with in Coton de Tulear breed to preserve this genetic combination. The result is the fine appearance of Coton de Tulear we see nowadays!

It is worthy of mention that the Coton de Tulear breed is known to be of the Bichon type. It is possibly related to the French Bichon and Italian Bolognese breeds, which explains its hairy look.

Another matter of concern revolving around the presence of Coton de Tulear is that it was revived from extinction.

Alternatively, some experts say that the breed that became extinct in the eastern part of Madagascar was a distant cousin of the Coton de Tulear which held remarkable resemblance.

This means the history of Coton de Tulear in fact stretches back a couple of centuries with little recognition outside the realms of Madagascar.

The last two decades, however, have been particularly illuminating for the Coton de Tulear breed. Not only has the breed been recognized by several renowned dog clubs (or is under the process of official recognition) around the world but has also been imported by several countries.

The breed is now available in almost every country!

# Chapter 3: Breeding

Most of what the dog becomes depends on how it is bred. This phenomenon stays true for all dog breeds. It is the fundamental stage to ensure the health and well-being of a dog.

Breeding dogs is a tricky process as it involves taking care of several intricacies at once. Contrary to popular belief, simply having a male and a female dog does not suffice in ensuring healthy puppies. A lot more needs to be done!

So if you are looking for the companionship of happy healthy Coton de Tulear dogs, your quest should instead begin with locating genuine breeders!

A person who knows how to go about the procedure is in a better state to not only provide you with purebred and healthy puppies but also guide you at every stage of dog ownership.

Here is how you can establish whether the breeder you are looking at is really a good one or not. Make sure you do not rush through the selection phase, as it is pivotal to your relationship with your pet!

## *1) Establishing a Reputable Breeder*

Every person operating a dog farm or being in possession of a dog litter is not a reputable breeder. Before you go hunting for your perfect pet, it is important to establish where and what you need to be looking for.

If you are doing this right, there are fewer chances your project will go wrong anywhere along the way.

Remember, the breeder is pivotal in deciding how healthy or long-lived your canine will be. There is nothing you can do about an erroneous genetic code so you would be better off staying away from it!

A genuine breeder knows how to breed the best quality pedigrees. So once you've found the breeder, you have already landed yourself a jackpot!

There are quite a few reputable Coton de Tulear breeders in the world. A quick Internet research will lead you to the closest one in your vicinity.

However, be smart about your research online as it is much easier to conduct fraud online than it is to do in the physical world.

It is important that you check and double check for the integrity of the breeder – whether online or from a referral. It is best to make your purchase from authentic Coton de Tulear clubs or associated members only.

Ask for their association/registration if you think it is necessary or it will help you identify fraud. Also, check out a few references to be absolutely sure about your choice.

When it comes to interrogating references, never hold back any questions. It is not exactly difficult to conjure up references that will never say a word against the breeder.

Never rely on telephonic conversations or those in which face-to-face interaction is not present. Drive an additional mile to meet the owners and to make sure the Coton de Tulear dog they have purchased is what you would like to have in near future.

Also, never rely on a single interrogation. If you are willing to invest in a little extra at this point, rest assured the outcome in a few years will be highly likeable.

Also, make sure you prompt the breeder about health documents. Seek the health certifications of the dogs used for breeding and also ask for any documents (vaccinations etc) that may be available for the litter. A genuine breeder would keep these records in order at all times!

Most professional breeders will require you to sign a document – a contract – before you take your newfound canine friend away from their premises. It is a normal procedure followed by most breeders. Make sure you have read the fine print thoroughly.

Most authentic breeders will allow you to return the pet in case it does not fit in with your family or you are no longer capable of caring for it. It will then be adopted by another family if appropriate.

However, if there is no-return policy, you might want to rethink your decisions about purchasing the dog.

In a similar way, there are other factors that play a pivotal role in determining the authenticity of the breeder. There may be a few more hidden conditions written in the fine print. This is the part that you need to read carefully.

You will automatically realize those pointers which protect the breeders unnecessarily. Deliberate on these points before giving your consent!

Do everything within your capacity to establish the authenticity of the breeder. There is also a list of questions you should ask the breeder before finalizing the deal (covered a little later).

On the same note, there are quite a few questions you can expect the breeder to ask you to see how serious you are about petting a Coton de Tulear dog.

## 2) Meeting its Parents

Meeting the mother and father of your new Coton de Tulear puppy can tell you a great deal about what the temperament and demeanor of your puppy will likely be when they grow into fine adults.

The Coton de Tulear puppy's personality or temperament will be a combination of what they experience in the early days of their environment when they are in the breeder's care, and the genes inherited from both parents.

Visiting the breeder several times, observing the parents, interacting with the puppies and asking plenty of questions will help you to get a true feeling for the sincerity of the breeder.

The early environment provided by the breeder and the parents of the puppies can have a formative impact on how well your puppy will ultimately behave as an adult dog.

Meeting the parents of your pet will help you get a better idea about what to expect from your association. However, it cannot be considered as a guarantee for a successful relationship.

If the parents are not present on site (or if you are unable to get in touch with them for any reason), ask as many questions from the breeder as you can to analyze their temperament. Don't forget to ask about their health and medical records.

Documentation and registration papers are another method of analyzing the well-being of your new companion and its parents. This will be covered in ample detail later on!

## 3) The Questions to Ask Yourself

Choosing the <u>right</u> puppy for your family and your lifestyle is more important than you might imagine.

Many people do not give serious enough thought to sharing their home with a new puppy before they actually bring one home.

For instance, many of us choose a puppy solely based on what it looks like, because the breed may currently be popular, or because their family had the same kind of dog when they were growing up.

Here are some of the important questions you need to ask yourself before you proceed further with the acquisition process.

In order to be fair to ourselves, our family and the puppy we choose to share our lives with, we humans need to take a serious look at our life, both as it is today and what we envision it being in the next ten to fifteen years, and then ask ourselves a few important personal questions and honestly answer them, before making the commitment to a puppy! These include:

1. Do I have the time and patience necessary to devote to a puppy, which will grow into a great dog that needs a great deal of attention, training and endless amounts of my devotion?
The Coton de Tulear dog loves attention and usually gets anxious if left alone for long time periods. If you don't have the time or will to care for its diverse needs, you might not be well suited to pet the Coton de Tulear dog!

2. Do I lead a physically active, medium or low intensity life? For instance, am I out jogging the streets daily or climbing mountains or would I rather spend my leisure time on the couch?
The Coton de Tulear dogs are moderately active. They adjust well to the subtle indoors but would definitely love to get a long walk any time during the day!

3. Do I like to travel a lot?
If you do, do you think you can carry around the Coton de Tulear dog with you?
Generally, the Coton de Tulear is quite mobile owing to its small size and amiable nature. It can adjust well to car rides, air travel and every other form of transport. The end decision then lies upon you – are you willing to carry it around?
Do keep in mind that carrying around a dog usually means you will need to carry around quite a few supplies with it. That is the package deal!

4. Am I a neat freak?

Another way to put this question is; can I tolerate the mess created by the puppy?

The Coton de Tulear dog is not a very heavy hair shedder. In fact, most people consider it as a non-shedding breed.

Despite this, its small size and inquisitive nature means it will be getting into a lot of places it shouldn't be and might even be creating trouble.

5. Do I have a young, growing family that takes up all my spare time?

A dog needs a lot of time and attention. If you are too busy or occupied with other tasks, your Coton de Tulear dog will feel neglected. At some point, it may even give rise to behavioral problems!

6. Am I physically fit and healthy enough to be out there walking a dog?

Try to be realistic while answering this question. Most people find it difficult to admit they are not up for strenuous activities till the reality finally dawns upon them somehow.

The Coton de Tulear dog needs a moderately active and fit partner. It wouldn't be much of a problem walking the Coton de Tulear.

However, it does enjoy hiking too!

7. Can I afford the food costs and the veterinarian expenses that are part of being a conscientious dog guardian?

The Coton de Tulear dog cannot be considered cheap. It is a moderately expensive breed when it comes to acquisition, training and development, grooming and upkeep!

An estimate is given subsequently in this book. Look it through and then decide wisely!

8. Is the decision to bring a puppy into my life a family decision, or just for the children, who will quickly lose interest?

If it is just the children's decision, who will take care of the Coton de Tulear dog once the kids lose interest in keeping up with its needs?

It is always better if bringing a dog home is based on a responsible adult's decision! That way, the association is likely to last long and be fruitful!

9. Have I researched the breed I'm interested in? And is it compatible with my lifestyle?

Incompatibility will naturally disrupt the whole point of association.

If you are looking for a truly memorable relationship with your canine, compatibility is the first thing you should be looking for!

10. What is the number one reason why I want a dog in my life?

You need a better answer than just "I feel like it" or "Because I want it"!

Have an answer which translates into a lasting relationship and not just a short term infatuation!

Once you ask yourself these important questions and honestly answer them, you will have a much better understanding of the type of puppy that would be best suited for you and your family, and whether or not, it should be a Coton de Tulear dog.

If you are too busy for a dog, or choose the wrong dog, you will inevitably end up with an unhappy dog, which will lead to behavioral issues, which then will lead to an unhappy family and extra expense to hire a professional to help you reverse unwanted behavioral problems. Please take the time to choose wisely.

If you have absolutely decided that the Coton de Tulear is the right dog for you, here are some of the questions you should ask the breeder to ensure you are making the right purchase.

## 4) *The Questions to Ask the Breeder*

Before making your investment, you are allowed to ask as many questions to the breeder as possible – even to the point of irritating the breeder.

It is your right to put all your concerns at peace before making the purchase. Be absolutely sure about the specimen and its quality so you can share a mutually beneficial bonding later on.

It is always a good idea to read up about the dog breed you are planning to have. NEVER go to the breeder with absolutely no idea about what is it that you want or what it is that you are looking for.

Trade frauds are really not very uncommon. Knowledge is the only thing that can keep you safe from it.

Do not give in to the allegations put forth by the breeder. Even if there is something you do not know about, make sure you do not make it evident to the breeder. If you do, it will automatically give the breeder a license to bombard you with lies and false claims.

Take time to prepare yourself before heading off to the breeder. In fact, it is best to get information from multiple breeders and a handful of their customers before making the final purchase decision.

Keep in mind these decisions cannot be reversed as easily as you would like to do if and when you realize the plan has backfired. Even if you are approaching a breeder through reference, it is still important to make sure all your questions have been appropriately answered.

On this note, it is worthy of being mentioned that all breeders are not operating simply to rob you of your finances or to deliver low quality canine friends that fail to behave the way they are supposed to!

You might be one of the lucky ones to come across a breeder who is actually helpful in guiding you towards the selection. While it is important to keep your guard up and not rely completely on the breeder, it is not entirely impossible that the breeder will have some valuable insight for you.

Know what you need to say and when. Don't come off as a stubborn know-it-all or as an ignorant person. Strike a balance – keep your eyes, ears and mind open.

Prepare well so you are in a better state to identify fraud when and if it happens.

Here is a list of questions that you should ask the breeder in order to evaluate his/her authenticity.

Quite obviously, the focus here is interrogating the breeder about a Coton de Tulear puppy instead of a full grown dog. But it is sufficient to give you an idea of what all you need to know.

Any questions you think are equally applicable on the dog can be asked as it is. If there are other concerns on your mind, discuss and clear those as well.

You do not want to enter into a dog companionship with doubt on your mind!

1. How long have you been involved with the Coton de Tulear breed? How many litters have you witnessed and grown?
The longer and the more litters the breeder has worked with, the better it will be. This means the breeder has ample hands-on experience and will therefore know all pros and cons of the breed. At a future date, you will be able to use this expertise to your own benefit as well.

2. Why do you breed Coton de Tulear dogs in particular?
Look for a satisfactory answer beyond the usual gibberish. It should strike to you as satisfactory.
There are no hard and fast rules to determine which answer is to be considered appropriate or which should not. If there is a story behind this association, show your interest and curiosity about it!

3. How frequently is the litter expected?
Too frequent breeding means the quality of the puppies is being compromised.
Too many litters from the same female Coton de Tulear dog means it is not being adequately cared for and is likely to face declining health.
Healthy kids are usually not born to an unhealthy mother.

4. Who were the parents for the puppy?
It doesn't matter if they are not present on site; ask for images and medical records for both parents.
If the breeder is able to show you pictures of relatives, make a mental record for these as well. These will come in handy later on while further identifying the authenticity of the breed.

5. Where and how are the puppies kept?
Make a mental note of the sanitation facilities, cleanliness, environment, availability of space and all other factors present on site. This is what the puppy is accustomed to.
If you cannot offer something close to this environment, you can expect all sorts of "cute" tantrums from your Coton de Tulear pet as it adjusts in to the new environment.

6. What are the most common problems associated with the Coton de Tulear breed?
Although admittedly the prevalence of problems in Coton de Tulear dogs is quite rare, experts agree that a breeder who has witnessed a minimum of two litters will definitely experience some problem or the other.
It does not have to be a major health complication. Any information that suggests the breeder has in fact witnessed multiple generations will suffice.

7. Are the parents certified?
Have a look at the certifications offered by the breeder, if any. If you come across the AKC or The Kennel Club of UK papers, rest assured the puppy will be healthy and happy.

As for other documents, take your time to identify if there are actually genuine or not.

8. Do you have any kennel club memberships?
Most clubs have strict rules about how the canines are cared for. So if there is a reputed club membership involved, you can rest assured the puppies will be adequately cared for.
This is not a necessity. The presence of membership documents is a plus point – its lack thereof cannot really be considered as a negative!

9. Can I see the medical records for this puppy?
Make sure all the documents are in order – especially those pertaining to shots and vaccinations.
If there are any other "special" cases involved, make sure you ask as much about it as you would like to know. Better to be informed beforehand what you are headed into.

10. Can I see the contract before signing?
Take special care to read the fine print between the lines. Inquire about individual clauses mentioned about the transfer of ownership.
Make sure you have inquired about the return policy to protect yourself from future troubles.
Anything that does not seem right is most probably not so – either have the clause changed or find another breeder.

11. What is involved in the guarantee cover?
Look for pointers about a return policy, medical coverage, exchange policy and everything else mentioned in there. You need to be fully aware of the options available to you given the association does not work out.
The contingency needs to be planned before the transfer or you will be left with no choice but to put up with something that does not meet with your expectations!

12. Can I have references of your customers?
A breeder that shies away from sharing this information is

definitely one that is questionable. Most reputed dog breeders will have this information readily available.

Take your time to inquire about the canines from these customers before returning to make the purchase. Witness the specimen with your eyes and don't believe on verbal stories – the latter can be concocted quite easily!

13. Do you have any records of participating in dog events?
It will promote the authenticity of the breeder. If the breeder has participated in dog events, it is most likely to be genuine since all breeders do not survive the tough scrutiny conducted by the event managers.

14. Do you have experience dealing with this single breed or multiple ones?
If the breeder is known to have switched between different dog breeds from time to time, it definitely points towards instability and inexperience.

Look for someone who depicts consistency. Breed switching is almost a sure guarantee the breeder does not know how to handle the dogs!

15. Were the parents of the puppy scrutinized for dog diseases?
Look for detailed records that include investigating dysplasia, luxating patella, optical health, heart problems, seizures, epilepsy, allergies, thyroid problems, congenital issues, and all other possible problems.

The AKC papers and the Kennel Club of UK registration papers will have enough information about the parents' medical problems. If you have got your hands on these, rest assured these will be reliable and accurate.

As far as other documents are concerned, you will need to do your research to find out which ones are genuine.

16. When was the puppy separated from the mother and fellow litter?
If the breeder quotes duration shorter than eight weeks, it is likely to have behavioral problems that will make handling more

difficult. This is because the basic value exchange occurs while the puppy is still under the mother's care.

Early separation means the value exchange is incomplete. Such puppies are known to have personality issues that make handling difficult.

17. When will the puppy be ready for a ride home?
It is normal to keep the puppy intact with the mother for a minimum of seven to eight weeks. Even after this period, some time will be needed to acclimatize it to foreign environments.
If the breeder seems to be in a hurry to get rid of the puppy, this is definitely the sign that raises suspicion!

18. How and when was the first Coton de Tulear couple imported?
As mentioned previously, this species is specific to Madagascar. Anyone who says the breed is locally (other than in Madagascar) promoted definitely has no knowledge of the breed's origin.
Make sure the breeder can trace back the lineage to Madagascar or you will end up settling for another breed in the name of Coton de Tulear dogs.

19. How are the puppies socialized?
Find out what was done to encourage puppies to socialize. The first lessons they learn usually come from their littermates.
If something else has been done (training etc) to promote socialization, make a mental note of it. This will definitely help you later on when you are trying to get the pet to adjust to your rules!

20. Has the puppy itself or anyone of its siblings been reported sick?
Keep in mind that the genetic code is similar for all littermates. A problem with one can almost certainly be expected with another. If the breeder is hesitant, feel free to ask for medical documents pertaining to other littermates.

21. How many visits to the veterinary doctor have been made?
Seek medical reports for each visit. Any discrepancy is supposed to be looked upon with distrust.

22. What all does the puppy eat to meet its nutritional requirement?
Make a list of all the things it is known to tolerate well so you know what to feed it.
Some dogs/puppies may be accustomed to special meals. It is best to know this beforehand so you can conduct its preliminary shopping according to its wishes.

23. Describe a typical day in the life of the puppy.
It will give you sufficient insight about the activity level and demands of the pet.
Inquire about the shady areas to fully understand your puppy's needs. You definitely do not want surprises waiting for you at the other end!

24. What should I take care of as the owner?
Also, inquire if you will be given continued assistance even after the contract has been signed.
A responsible breeder will be more concerned about the puppy's health rather than money and will therefore be available whenever you face any problems.
If s/he isn't, it is most probably because they are not well aware of the breed!

25. What are the best training methods to be used for this breed?
A person who has devoted significant amount of time handling the specific breed will know the answer.
If the breeder is being too ambiguous or vague, it points towards inexperience and lack of knowledge.

26. How often will the puppy need to be groomed?
Again, the experienced breeder will be in a better state to give you an appropriate answer to this.
Hope to hear about its non-shedding nature and about **why** it

needs to be groomed daily.
One word answers like "Daily" or "Weekly" is not really the
answer you are looking for at this point!

27. How large will the puppy get?
Coton de Tulear dogs normally do not grow much in size unless
they are a specific genetic variation. If the breeder cannot say so,
s/he is most probably new to the breed.
It goes without saying that the breeder in this case is not the one
you should be looking for!

28. Does the specific breed get along well with other animals?
This might be handy if you already have or plan to adopt more
pets.
Coton de Tulear dogs, generally, do not welcome competition
nicely. If the breeder fails to give this fact adequate emphasis, it is
most probably because s/he is trying to get rid of the dogs. It
should spark concern for your personal safety.

29. Can it be left alone?
There is no single word answer to this question.
Specifically about the Coton de Tulear breed, the breeder should
deliberate about the energy reserve, the exercise requirement, the
need for attention and the subsequent time span it can be left
alone.
If the breeder is hesitant about sharing this information, there is
definitely something wrong with the puppy in question.

30. Has the puppy been micro-chipped or tattooed?
It will simply be good to know about it beforehand. It is not a
prerequisite.
Micro-chipping, however, might make it easier for you to locate
your pet if it decides to take off into the wild in any direction!

If there are any other concerns or questions in your mind, feel free
to inquire about them. Adopting a pet or living with one is not
easy. You definitely want to be absolutely sure about your
choices before you have made them.

Your search for a responsible, genuine and reputable breeder does not end when you have received proper answers to these questions. The good ones want their puppies to go into good homes where they can settle down with ease.

So while you inquire about the breeder's authenticity, be prepared to be questioned in return so the breeder knows how serious you are about petting the Coton de Tulear dog. The next section covers this part in adequate detail.

## 5) The Questions to Expect From the Breeder

The breeders will also want to ensure you are the right owner for the puppy available for adoption. So you should anticipate the breeder to ask the following questions from you too!

If s/he doesn't, the odds are high that the business is solely being run for profit and the breeder has no regard for the family or the well-being of the puppy whatsoever. Naturally, this means trouble as the money-minded breeder will seldom take responsibility for things that do not work out.

This also means they will have no regard for the puppy's well being either on their own site or in the adopter's home. Amidst the rising number of frauds and reckless behavior, you can play your role by at least selecting the breeder responsibly!

Here is what they should ask you:

1. What kind of a lifestyle do you have – laid back, athletic or somewhere in the middle?
It is important to match the personality of the dog with the personality of the owner for a problem-free association. A mismatch in this regard can result in serious disasters for both. It is not unnatural for the breeder to be interested in your day-to-day activities. If your activity level is not adequately matched with the moderately energetic nature of the Coton de Tulear dog, the breeder should be able to warn you beforehand!

2. Any prior experiences with dogs/puppies?

Experience works both ways.

An experienced breeder can help you make intelligent dog choices.

An experienced owner, such as you, can help the puppy feel at home and transit seamlessly from the breeder's space to the new abode.

After all, it is the puppy that is at the center of the equation. Everything that is being done is to ensure the little ones get the right homes where they can thrive!

3. Are there any small children or other animals involved in the scenario?

They do impact the way the new addition to the family will react or adjust to the environment.

New pets around very small children are not encouraged for obvious reasons and the Coton de Tulear is no exception to this. So if there are any small children that your new acquisition is required to settle in with, an untrained Coton de Tulear dog might not be the best choice.

4. Where do you live?

The Coton de Tulear breed in particular does not have problems with the apartment life. Even the backyard is not important though these qualities may be a must for some other specific breeds.

The responsible breeder will want to match up the dog's requirement with the resources available to make sure the puppy's care is not compromised.

It is best not to feign answers just to get the Coton de Tulear puppy – for all you know you might have to put it out at a later date because the canine fails to behave properly.

5. What is the purpose of the adoption?

The breeder will want to know if s/he is dealing with competition or with the final consumer.

If your adoption motives include raising a family dog, the breeder might mandate you to neuter or spay the animal (covered later) for its own health.

In other cases, the dealing will be substantially different.

In either case, don't hesitate to share your motives. For all you know you might end up with sterilized pairs of Coton de Tulear dogs which will be of no use when it comes to breeding and procreation!

6. What do you know about this breed?

Well, the breeder wants to know if you are up for the challenges faced while bringing up the Coton de Tulear breed. S/he would test your knowledge just to be sure you are aware about it.

Make sure you have done your research well or at least have some witty answers prepared to compel the breeder to talk.

If you come off as someone purchasing the Coton de Tulear dog for no good reason, it might make them rethink their decisions.

7. Are you aware of the costs?

Most first timers will not have any idea. Let the breeder educate you about the costs involved with maintaining a pet.

Apart from the substantial chunk that goes into its medical bills, the daily expenditure is also not child's play. Be mentally prepared for it all.

A general estimate for the upkeep of a Coton de Tulear dog is given later on this book. Go through that to get an idea how the finances work.

The bottom line is a responsible breeder wants the puppy to go into a good home and you would like a companion you can settle easily with. Lies will only make the matters worse – for all participants.

It is best to be honest in this exchange for the benefit of all three parties involved – the breeder, the new owner and the poor little fellow whose fate is being decided!

Although you wouldn't want to come off as someone who is too laid back to help with the puppy's chores, faking answers will be of no help when the chores are actually thrust upon you.

It is therefore crucial for everyone to participate productively –
for everyone's mutual benefit. After all, it is about a decade long
association – sometimes even more so!

It needs to be peaceful for all three parties involved to maximize
the returns multifold.

## 6) Selecting the Right Puppy From the Litter

Just as every person born in this world is different and unique, so
is every puppy.

They have their own individual personalities slightly different
from others. All puppies belonging to a specific dog breed are not
identical. In fact, such consistency doesn't exist even among
puppies from the same litter!

This is why most often breeders dedicate extra time to match the
puppy with the family.

However, the selection phase is not that simple. At times there
may be several other factors governing your decision to purchase
a specific puppy.

For instance, you may feel particularly drawn towards a specific
puppy in contrast to others. However, you need to be smarter
about your choices for better associations.

At times, you may feel drawn to rescue a pet simply because it
looks too depressed. As a natural human instinct, you would want
to "save" it from an unfortunate fate. Unless you have prior
experience handling dogs, such an action is strictly not
recommended.

Such dogs usually have behavioral issues which can prove to be
extremely challenging to handle. Such a dog usually doesn't go
down alone but takes the whole family along.

On the same note, keep in mind that minor behavioral problems can be resolved by training provided it is started off during the early months. As the time passes, the dog's personality and habits become too stubborn to be modified.

Evaluate your decision wisely before settling for any one puppy. Moreover, here are some other pointers that will help you identify a well-behaved puppy from the lot.

Make a special note about the puppy's social activities, with those of its own kind and of another breed (if available on site). Here is what you should be looking out for.

1. Are the dogs active and playful? If they are playing tug of war, which puppy particularly likes being on the top at all times? Is there a particular dog that plays well with either position? These ones are the ones you should opt for since they are more likely to be well-behaved when they grow up.

2. Do the dogs have toys to play with? Is there a particular dog that seems to be too possessive about its toys and will keep other dogs away from his toys? If so, this means trouble. Such a dog is likely to be too possessive – even for its owner. Behavioral problems and training difficulties will eventually follow.

3. Is there a particular dog which likes to remain aloof and away from the pack? If a puppy doesn't like the company of its littermates, it is least likely to enjoy the company of a human. The association will be looked upon as intrusion on the personal space and hence problems will follow. You are definitely not looking for an anti-social puppy.

4. While playing, puppies do bite each other. It is quite normal for them. However, what you need to be looking out for is this; when and if a puppy bites another one and the other cries out or yelps, is the biter quick in releasing the grasp? Puppies that known when to loosen up when the other puppy is in pain will respond well when humans are present in the victim's place.

5. Is the puppy you are hoping to buy sociable with people? Does it blend in well with people or does it start growling and pawing at people? Or does it get frightened and draws back into a secluded corner?
You are looking for a social dog that will blend in well with people, especially you. Make your decisions wisely.

Make sure you handle the puppy only at the time it is acting responsibly. If you pick a puppy while it is growling or acting defensively, you will reinforce its negative behaviors and hence fall prey to future problems.

Make sure you seek the puppy's health records as well. Observe closely to see whether the puppy is able to walk properly, listen properly, see properly and perform other basic activities with precision.

If it is facing any kind of difficulty, get it checked with the veterinarian at the earliest. More so, you can even ask the breeder to get the veterinarian doctor on board before signing the deal.

On the same note, here are some on the physical characteristics of healthy Coton de Tulear dogs. However, keep in mind that these evaluations are extremely unprofessional on your behalf.

These characteristics might be able to highlight major problems with the dog but the veterinary doctor is the most appropriate person to diagnose further problems. This analysis cannot be considered as a suitable alternative for your puppy's first visit to the veterinary doctor!

1. Breathing: normal healthy dogs will breathe silently without exerting any apparent effort. If the puppy coughs, sneezes, or has certain unexplained discharges from the nose or the mouth, it most certainly means trouble.

2. Body: the puppy needs to look a little rounded and well fed instead of a frail figure struggling to walk properly. If you observe the latter, it most surely means the breeder is not doing a good job with the litter.

3. Coat: the Coton de Tulear normally has a long and soft coat. Make sure it is the same when you purchase it. There should be no dullness, greasiness, bald spots, dandruff or other explained symptoms.

4. Energy: let's just say the puppy should be excited to see you. If it seems too laid back or lethargic, you are most probably looking at a diseased or unkempt dog.

5. Hearing: if you clap your hands or blow the trumpet and experience no response from the puppy whatsoever, the only logical explanation for this is that it can probably not hear!

6. Genitals: a healthy puppy will generally not have any unexplained discharges around the sensitive areas.

7. Walking: is the puppy able to stand up straight without wobbling knees? Can it strut around happily and jump around obstacles with ease? If not, it most probably will have some kind of orthopedic issues.

8. Sight: if something moves within their field of vision and they do not follow it, it is most probably because they cannot see it. Look for any discharges from the eyes or any spots therein. Get an opinion from the veterinary doctor as well.

Then again, keep in mind that this cannot be substituted for the puppy's initial visit to the veterinary doctor! Do keep your eyes open and observe closely. Seek professional help as and when required.

# Chapter 4: Physical Characteristics

If you have read through the previous section thoroughly and decided that the Coton de Tulear dog is indeed the dog you are looking for, the next step is to proceed with the acquisition.

But what exactly are you looking for? You need to be aware of the Coton de Tulear dog's appearance so you do not end up purchasing another breed in its name. The small fluffy appearance of the Coton de Tulear can be seen across quite a few dog breeds.

Here is what you need to know about the Coton de Tulear's physical appearance and characteristics to identify the true breed.

## *1) Their Origin*

As mentioned previously, Coton de Tulear is the Royal dog of Madagascar. How it came to be in this part of the world is the topic for another debate (which by the way has been discussed previously)!

The Coton de Tulear is genetically linked with the French Bichon as these are the most likely ancestors for this breed. Its apparent outlook seems to be close to the Italian Bolognese breed as well. However, the former is the most likely predecessor.

The breed gained popularity after the French invasion of Madagascar which most surely points towards the fact that the Coton de Tulear belongs to the French Bichon. At the same time, it is believed half of the genetic combination has been contributed by the local breed of Madagascar, which has now become extinct.

The breed has probably survived for several hundreds of years. Despite this, it was officially recognized more or less about two decades ago.

The breed is local to Madagascar, yet it is present in almost all parts of the world. This was made possible through import and export of this breed across geographical boundaries.

Here is the catch – the breed has adapted to the local environments in different parts of the world. This means the physical characteristics of standard Coton de Tulear in the United States and the United Kingdom will be slightly different than Madagascar.

The formation of standard guidelines is therefore a source of contempt amidst several different parties who have their interests vested in this breed.

## 2) *Salient Physical Features*

As mentioned previously, there is no singular universally accepted standard that defines a Coton de Tulear. Slight variations exist. We will try to get the best possible outline for the physical characteristics of the Coton de Tulear and also mention the known variations that fall within acceptable parameters. So here it goes!

The most noticeable physical characteristic about the Coton de Tulear is its hair. The texture of its hair is such that it cannot be classified as the fur. The hairs are extremely soft to touch, long and have striking resemblance to cotton. Hence the name!

Other important physical characteristics include black rounded eyes peeping in from the mass of hair on its face. If the hair is not groomed on a daily basis, there is a chance its eyes might not be visible to the naïve observer at all.

Its eyes are lively, bright and intelligent. It may be framed by dark colored skin. As the cuddlesome creature peers from behind the bangs, it looks even more endearing!

A small but prominent black nose sits on the tip of its muzzle. Beneath its nose, you will find a rather small jaw. The skin on its lips is tight and usually black in color though white colored lips are also quite common. Unlike other dog breeds, the lips are stretched tightly over its teeth which give it a strangely playful appearance.

The Coton de Tulear is generally a small breed that has short legs – even in proportion to its body size. However, in some parts of the world, you might come across exceptionally tall Coton. In fact, tall Coton can be born to perfectly normal sized parents as well.

It is believed to be the matter of genetic combination for the Coton de Tulear which defines its height and weight. It is possible that the local dog breed of Madagascar with which the French Bichon mated were slightly taller. The code therefore runs within the Coton de Tulear breed as a recessive gene.

It has short legs. The forelegs are completely covered by the mass of hair on its body. The hind legs may be slightly visible despite the hair. Usually, the forelegs do not have a lot of muscle which does not really explain its sprightly nature or its stamina!

It has a well rounded skull though it is completely hidden under the hair. The muzzle is small and slightly tapered though there is a visible depression at the point where the muzzle begins.

As far as its ears are concerned, they are proportionately sized according to its skull and drop slightly on either side of its face. However, due to the hair on its hair, the ears may appear to be larger than they really are.

More so, they blend in perfectly with the puppy's hairs all over the body. So it may appear not to have ears!

The hair growth is slightly denser on its chest just as it is on its chin and lips. The Coton de Tulear may appear to have a beard and a moustache! The puppy has a long sturdy neck supporting the skull. The hair seems to cover it all.

Its feet are rounded and usually black on the underside. They appear fuller and sturdier when compared with other hairy breeds.

It has a proportionate tail which is densely covered by hair. The tail may be held straight or slightly curved depending on the puppy's mood.

The overall appearance of the Coton de Tulear is that of a cotton ball. Except that it has life and jumps around the place on its own!

## *3) Coat Colors*

The Coton de Tulear dog's coat is the singularly most important aspect of its appearance. It comes in different colors.

It may be completely white in color, completely black, may have occasional marks or may even be tricolor. In addition to this, keep in mind that the coat of the Coton de Tulear is likely to change colors throughout its life.

For instance, as the puppy reaches adulthood, a significant change in its coat color may occur. It is not uncommon for purely white Coton dog's to get marks around different parts of their body as they grow. It usually happens around the ears though it may happen on any part of its body.

Pure white Coton de Tulear dogs are generally preferred by the dog clubs and considered to be the purebreds. In dog shows and competitions all around the world, you will see Coton de Tulear dogs that have a pure white coat!

It may be for the reason that white Coton dogs have a certain attractive appeal about them which makes them look more dazzling that tricolor ones.

The coat has a distinctive "hair" feel to it instead of the typical dog fur. This does not mean the hair will cling onto each other and appear like nodules or small bunches of hair. It should appear as though it has been brushed through air! This is the sign of a healthy coat.

## 4) Height and Weight

The Coton de Tulear is a small breed. It fits into your arms perfectly and hence is extremely portable.

On average, the Coton de Tulear dog's height ranges between 8 and 12 inches. Its weight ranges between 8 and 13 pounds.

The Federation Cynologique Internationale (FCI) states the standard for Coton de Tulear as follows: The male Coton de Tulear has a height between 9.8 and 11.8 inches while the female one stands 8.7 to 10.6 inches tall. Similarly, the former weighs between 8.8 to 13.2 pounds while the latter weighs between 7.7 and 11 pounds!

The Coton de Tulear Club of America differs slightly. It states the standards for this breed as follows: Irrespective of gender, the Coton de Tulear is likely to have a height between 9 and 13 inches and weigh somewhere between 11 and 15 pounds!

The Coton de Tulear Club of America also recognizes the standard for Tall Coton de Tulear dogs. According to it, the tall Coton de Tulear can have a height between 15 and 17 inches.

Although tall Coton de Tulear dogs are a rarity, this cannot be considered as a disqualification from the breed.

The typical dimension of the Coton dog is the main reason why it is considered as a small companion dog or toy dog by most dog clubs around the world!

## 5) *Life Expectancy*

Most small dog breeds have exceptionally long drawn life spans. Same is the case with the Coton de Tulear.

On average, the Coton de Tulear relationship lasts for about 14 years at the minimum. The upper limit of this range can be 16 to 20 depending on how well you take care of your puppy.

If its nutritional and health needs are being fulfilled properly, the Coton de Tulear will survive for a long time.

Even though this is seldom a concern amidst true dog enthusiasts, it doesn't hurt to have an idea how long do you have to make memories that will last forever!

## 6) *Litter Size*

On average, the Coton de Tulear produces 5 littermates at a time. In some cases, the number may be larger or smaller depending on the mother.

## 7) *Personality*

The Coton dog generally has an impressive personality. With its hairy exterior and in-built grace, this particular breed is a popular participant in almost all dog shows.

It usually holds its neck high in a sprightly position. It can be seen shuffling its small legs and paws rapidly in order to keep up with the pace of its leader.

The tightened lips make it appear as though it is smiling at all times. Coupled with the bright shiny eyes, the dog seems to be in a good mood! So its playful activities look more charming to the eye.

The Coton de Tulear has a habit of cheering up its owner in any way possible. So if you suddenly see the Coton de Tulear jumping back on its hind legs and trotting around with hilarious pride, it is most probably because it wants to please you!

The Coton de Tulear is generally considered to be an amiable dog fit to be taken in as a companion. It demands attention but does not really have many exhaustive needs. So if you have a laid back lifestyle, the Coton de Tulear will prove to be the right dog for you!

You can easily show it off to your social circle and take pride in being its owner. It is not just dazzlingly beautiful but quite intelligent too!

## 8) Intelligence

The Coton de Tulear is regarded as one of the most intelligent dog breeds. As said previously, the dog has beauty along with brains that makes it the complete package. The Coton de Tulear is easily trainable provided it gets the right leadership. It is important for the owner to be polite yet determined when s/he gives an instruction to the dog. This means the dominance issues will not arise knowing that the puppy is supposed to be subservient to its master!

Apart from this, the Coton de Tulear is a natural entertainer. It knows a couple of tricks that it uses quite often to entertain the owner. A few others can easily be taught to the puppy through a little training and role playing. It is a sight to behold to see the Coton de Tulear trotting on its hind legs in a human-like way Moreover, the Coton de Tulear is known to be a rapid learner. It can memorize gestures with ease. All that you need to do is repeat the gestures twice or thrice in front of the little puppy and it will be able to do so with quite some precision the third time!

This also translates into trouble though. If there is a particular action that you do not want your Coton de Tulear to perform, it is better not to teach it. The Coton de Tulear has a knack of thinking out of the box. So there are chances the newly learned trick might be used for the owner's detriment rather than entertainment.

If you put the Coton de Tulear through a maze, it will mostly probably be able to emerge victorious around the other end. It has problem solving and analytical capabilities which help it overcome an obstacle with ease.

The Coton de Tulear is also blessed with a photographic memory. It can therefore indentify even the smallest changes in the environment. This makes the Coton dcautious about its moves. It would look up to the owner to seek approval for its movements and then move forward with it even if it is absolutely sure about the action expected from it.

It observes patterns closely and learns from them. This helps it deduce solutions to different problems. This aspect also makes this breed easier to train with the right form of instruction.

The Coton de Tulear responds exceptionally well to positive behavior reinforcement tactics like treats. This, by no means, intends to undermine the importance of leadership in training. Coton de Tulear dogs learn better when the information is conveyed to them clearly in a strong tone but in an amiable manner! The Coton de Tulear is extremely submissive. Some may interpret it as "asking a lot of questions" or "trying to establish its dominance". However, none is the case!

The Coton is highly attached to its owner and demands attention. It would try to do nothing that actually puts off the owner! This is why the dog may be seen hesitating in responding to situations. It seeks approval for its moves beforehand so it can stay away from trouble!

The Coton de Tulear dogs know when to execute specific tricks and to make the most of these. Don't be surprised if they try to attract your attention if you are too busy with your guests.

They like being the center of attention and would do anything to achieve so – both when it comes to the owners as well as random observers! They make ideal playful companions. Do you still need more reasons to believe the breed is actually an intelligent one?

## 9) Preferred Living Conditions

The Coton de Tulear is a small and moderately active dog. It is therefore ideal for apartment life. It does not need a lot of space to settle in nor does it need a yard to exercise its energy effectively. Its activity level indoors will be quite sufficient to keep its disastrous streak to a bare minimum. Besides this, keep in mind that your Coton de Tulear dog will demand rigorous activity every once in a while. If you are planning to pet this dog, you will need to take it for weekly visits to the garden, on hikes or other forms of strenuous exercise to keep it fit and healthy.

This does not mean the Coton de Tulear is likely to fall ill if not taken on weekly hikes; it merely suggests that the Coton de Tulear likes this kind of activity. For the most part, the Coton de Tulear can adjust with the energy levels of its owners. This makes it a highly desirable canine companion for a lot of people.

## 10)   Other Vital Statistics

Here are a few other vital statistics you can expect to observe about your Coton de Tulear. This will help you recognize whether your Coton de Tulear is healthy or not.

1. Temperature: 100.5 to 102.5 degrees Fahrenheit (38.05 to 39.16 Celsius).

2. Respiratory Rate: 10 to 20 per minute.

3. Pulse: Puppies, 120 to 160 per minute. Adults, 60 to 140 per minute.

4. Gums: should be pink.

5. Eyes: should be clear and lively. No unexplained discharges to be tolerated.

# Chapter 5: Temperament

Once you are aware about the physical characteristics of the Coton de Tulear dog, the next thing you need to understand is the temperament for this little ball of fur. So here goes!

## *1) Is it a Workaholic?*

The Coton de Tulear is moderately active. It likes going around for walks and on hiking missions but would otherwise adjust well indoors as well. According to the precise definition of the word, the Coton de Tulear cannot be explained as a workaholic.

For the most part, the Coton cannot be assigned guarding duties. It does, however, have the tendency to respond to noises and begin barking in case it senses any imminent threat. However, this cannot be considered sufficient enough to ward off the threat.

Besides this, the main duty that your Coton is indeed capable of performing is to serve as your source of entertainment. It is a playful dog that can get overly excited by people's contributions. It likes being the center of attraction and will most probably do anything within its control to please its onlookers. It likes being in the company of humans and will become sad/depressed if kept alone.

Besides this, the Coton de Tulear can swim and follow its mounted owners. Despite its apparently small size, the Coton de Tulear has massive stamina and energy. Nevertheless, these activities cannot justify its role as a workaholic.

On the other hand, the Coton is known to adjust its energy levels to that of the owner. This means if you are a little towards the laid back type, the Coton de Tulear will also learn to rest more and be less active. For the most part, Coton may be described as a companion dog but not remotely as a workaholic.

## 2) *Behavior around Children*

The Coton de Tulear is known to blend well with people, especially children. It is gentle around babies. However, it is strongly recommended to put your Coton through relevant training courses to make sure it will not consider the naïve child as a threat. It is never a good idea to leave a dog alone with a baby or a small child.

As far as the initial interactions are concerned, it is best if these are conducted under the supervision of the owner. The Coton de Tulear may unintentionally harm the child while inspecting it curiously. For instance, the Coton de Tulear may try to bite in order to understand what the object is.

Although not recommended for extremely small children, the Coton de Tulear tends to grow on people over time. The Coton is likely to have an exceptionally good time trying to play with children. Once it is put through appropriate training and socialization courses, your dog will be ready to mingle with the little ones with ease!

## 3) *Behavior around Other Pets*

It is natural canine instinct to feel competitive in the company of other animals. They feel that other pets are competing for the owner's attention and hence are likely to act strangely in order to make the most of it. The Coton de Tulear is no exception to this.

As it is, the Coton tries to attract the owner's attention by walking on its hind legs or by performing certain tricks that they are well versed at. Although they are not likely to attack other pets, it is best to conduct the first interactions under supervision. Once the Coton de Tulear has registered the presence of other pets, it will blend in with them just as it does around the owner.

## 4) Is It An Escape Artist?

Attractive as it is, it is difficult to imagine how the amiable and cuddlesome Coton de Tulear would think about leaving its premises. This is where most people as mistaken.

The Coton de Tulear is an escape artist – but only when it is left alone for too long or if it is not allowed to come near its owners. If you try to lock this cuddlesome canine away while you have to run errands or go to the office, it is most likely to try and find its way out of captivity!

Popular signs of being an escape artist include the tendency of the Coton de Tulear to find its way around obstacles. So you need to put in barriers in order to contain it. However, with time, it will find a way to go around these barriers too. You will have to innovate continuously and find different ways to keep your little canine from getting away.

Another notable "habit" of the Coton de Tulear is its inclination to dig beneath fences. Seeing its size, it doesn't need a lot in order to get out. So if you are seeing unexplained heaps of mud around the area, it would be a good idea to scrutinize the area closely to see if your Coton de Tulear has been successful in building its escape route!

If your Coton de Tulear is adequately trained, exercised and disciplined, there is little reason to believe it will try to escape. On the whole, it is the perfect companion dog that you can have. However, if you haven't had the time to invest in its training or physical activity, being aware of its "escape artist" nature might pay off well.

A little care invested in time can save you from lots of trouble later on!

# Chapter 6: Evaluating the Pros and Cons

This brings us to the part where you get to analyze this breed for what it is and what it isn't. You need to know everything about this breed before you decide to buy it. This can save you from considerable heartbreaks later on!

Having a canine companion isn't a time-oriented passion; if you are in, you are in for decades at a time! Choose wisely so you don't have to put up your little companion up for adoption!

## *1) The Good Part about Coton de Tulear Ownership*

There are several benefits to Coton de Tulear ownership. Here are a few highlights to give you an idea:

1. The Coton de Tulear is **extremely adaptable**. It is well suited for the apartment lifestyle. It blends in well with families, small children and other pets given they don't feel threatened. They are also friendly towards strangers in general which makes it an ideal breed for people from all walks of life. However, people with athletic lifestyles won't be encouraged to get Coton de Tulear as their pet since the energy levels of this pet (comparative to athletes) will be low.

2. On the whole, the Coton de Tulear breed is very **friendly.** This can be gauged from the fact that it behaves well even in front of strangers. Its love for its owners is profound and can be witnessed through a number of activities it does to impress and entertain the onlookers. Besides this, its amiability can be observed by seeing how it reacts around kids and other pets. Nevertheless, training is a basic need to ensure your Coton de Tulear is amiable!

3. The Coton de Tulear can be **trained easily.** It is an intelligent breed which can self-learn most of the actions that it is required to do. For the most part, this breed seeks approval from its owner

before it moves forward with the activity. If you condition it to respect your words or signs, you will find it to be an extremely obedient dog.

4. It is **easy to groom** the Coton de Tulear dog. As it does not shed heavily, it therefore means you don't need to spend a lot of time removing hair from your possessions. If you are combing its hair on a periodic basis, there would be no leftovers on your property to clear up. The Coton de Tulear doesn't drool either, which is an added benefit to this breed.

5. **Less prone to health problems**. The Coton de Tulear does not fall prey to health problems very easily. In fact, there isn't any genetic health issues associated with this breed. Regular check up and vaccinations suffice to keep your dog healthy.

6. **Low Energy Levels** makes it easier to maintain the Coton de Tulear dog. As it does not have any strenuous exercise requirements, it can thrive with people who have extremely busy schedules. The miniature size coupled with low energy levels makes one-in-a-week visit to parks sufficient to keep it fit and healthy.

## *2) The Concerns over Coton de Tulear Ownership*

To this point, it is all fun and games. The Coton de Tulear might appear to be the perfect canine companion you can have. It definitely is one of the best ones there is. However, here are a few things you need to be aware of before you proceed with your purchase process.

1. It cannot be left alone for long. If it is required to stay alone for a couple of hours, it might behave well and not try to destroy your property. However, if it is left alone for prolonged periods of time, its destructive instincts come into perspective. It will try to claw and chew its way out of captivity. You need to be prepared for this kind of property loss if you are a frequent traveler or if you do not have the time to devote exclusively to your Coton de

Tulear dog. To resolve this problem, you can go for dog sitters, dog day cares and other similar options which makes someone in-charge of the house other than your puppy!

2. It cannot tolerate extreme temperatures. Well, it is a companion dog, not a guardian dog. For the most part, it cannot be left outdoors and certainly not when it is cold.

3. It might just be too friendly with the wrong kind of strangers. It doesn't bite often nor does it bark or howl. There are chances for your Coton de Tulear to become too friendly with everyone even if they are in to harm you physically or financially! It cannot protect you. So if you are looking for a guardian dog, the Coton de Tulear would be the worst decision you'd make.

4. Another important thing you need to be careful about is that your Coton de Tulear might be prone to the "small dog syndrome". Given its small size and playful behavior, you might end up overlooking quite a few outrageous behaviors on its behalf. This would reinforce negative traits in your Coton de Tulear which will pose difficulties later on when you decide to adopt other pets or "work against its will" in any way.

5. It is an escape artist. It will try to escape if it feels being captivated in any way. While doing so, it may cause considerable property damage as it tries to chew and wiggle through barriers. Make sure you don't leave its needs unattended. It may become quite a handful otherwise!

The Coton de Tulear breed traits have been foretold to you. Don't expect the dog to behave any different simply because you are its owner. It is best to assess these traits against your personality to make sure a match is made. It is the beginning of a remarkable journey!

# Chapter 7: The Acquisition Process

Now that you know everything that you need to know about the Coton de Tulear's personality and temperament, you are in a well-informed state to make the right decision. If the Coton de Tulear appears to be the right dog for you, then you should start worrying about where to buy one.

It begins by establishing a reputable breeder. If you are making an effort to get to the right breeder, you can expect your Coton de Tulear dog to behave like one. Cross breeding has greatly polluted the dog gene pool and has even increased the probability of genetic diseases.

In some cases, breeders mate their specimen so often that the litter becomes prone to several problems ranging for physical deformities to chronic health problems. If the mother is not cared for properly or is forced to produce litter too often, it affects her negatively. This effect is then transferred to the litter, which can create havoc for you!

It is best to look for a genuine breeder. If you find one in another city, don't hesitate to travel all the way there. You're better off with a Coton de Tulear dog that acts like one instead of a dog that is too raucous to tame!

Here are a few highlights you can use to identify where you'd be able to purchase your Coton de Tulear companion.

## 1) Where to Buy a Coton de Tulear in the US?

You've got a lot of options when it comes to the purchase decision. You can opt for private breeders, professional breeders, puppy farms and pet shops. Each medium has its own benefits and disadvantages. However, if you are not short on time or you are looking for a truly remarkable "investment", your chances lie with professional breeders.

In the United States, purchasing a Coton de Tulear dog and ensuring it is the right breed (or pure breed) is comparatively easy. This can be attributed to the fact that the Coton de Tulear is recognized by the AKC (American Kennel Club). In order to make sure you are getting the right deal, all you need to do is ask for the AKC papers.

The American Kennel Club is one of the most reputable dog clubs in the world. It safeguards pedigree breeds through registrations. The American Kennel Club was created with the idea to protect the sanctity of the dog gene pool. And it has been doing a commendable job for the past years.

The American Kennel Club can connect you with reputed breeders in your vicinity as well. Their website holds an elaborate breeder database which allows you to connect with the genuine breeders. This ensures your investment is secured.

If you are looking for breeders on your own, make sure you ask them for the AKC papers at least. The American Kennel Club registers pedigree breeds only. Even their documents are ample evidence for the genuineness of the breeder!

With online breeders and sellers, you need to be a little more careful. Make sure you've researched about the validity of your breeder. It is infinitely easier to conduct fraud online. Make sure you are not making any transfers before you've seen the dogs and their habitats for yourself. For one thing, Coton de Tulear dogs cannot be bred online – they have to have a physical existence somewhere!

To get an idea about what a Coton de Tulear is likely to cost you, read through the following sections carefully!

## 2) *Where to Buy a Coton de Tulear in the UK?*

The American Kennel Club operates in the United States and is considered as the primary evaluative measure there. In the United Kingdom, however, the AKC papers or registrations might not work as well.

In this part of the world, there is another important dog organization that is considered equivalent to the American Kennel Club. It is The Kennel Club. Like the American Kennel Club, the Kennel Club also recognizes Coton de Tulear as a unique breed. It is categorized as a toy dog given its size and activity levels. The thing about the Kennel Club is this – it registers mixed breeds as well. So you will find complete information about the orientation of your puppy whether it is a pure breed or not.

Just like in the United States, you will come across several private breeders, puppy farms, professional breeders and pet shops where the Coton de Tulear can be purchased from. If you are hoping to play a role in the protection of dog gene pool and you want to discourage unethical breeding habits, you are advised to go for professional breeders only. Also, seek affiliation records of these breeders with renowned dog clubs such as the Kennel Club. This will further ensure the breeder follows recommended guidelines properly.

If you are going for online breeders, take time to figure out whether they are genuinely authentic breeders or not. Most authentic ones do not resort to online selling. If they are, then it pays to dedicate some extra time to decide whether it is fraud or not. When and if you've made a financial transaction in their favor, rest assured they won't be reversed as easily!

## 3) *Estimated Prices for this Breed*

The next most important thing before you move forward with your Coton de Tulear dog purchase is to perform market research in order to find out the price of this breed. Every breeder will have their own cost. It is therefore best to look around a little and find the best fit for your lifestyle.

In the United States, the Coton de Tulear puppies cost between $600 and $1800. The cost will depend highly on the breeder's motives, the kind of puppy care offered and the age of the puppy. If the puppy is trained in advance, this will add cost to the price of the Coton de Tulear dog. Keep in mind that the price of your canine puppy has got nothing to do with its health or breed. Some professional breeders might offer their Coton de Tulear litter for extremely low prices given the buyer is truly enthusiastic about their dog. For them, the motive is to put the dogs in the right homes instead of making the most money out of their investment.

As for those residing in the United Kingdom, rest assured the Coton de Tulear is an expensive breed. In this part of the world, you might come across a Coton de Tulear puppy that costs you between £600 and £1,600. Then again, it depends on what the breeder is trying to achieve with this motive. If the breeder intends to put all littermates into the right homes, s/he will reduce cost significantly given the buyer exhibits the right kind of interest in the dog. Another case where the prices may be too low is when the breed isn't pure. Mixed breeds or unprofessionally bred littermates will often be sold for much cheaper to get them adopted as soon as possible.

Take your time to identify the breeder. The rest of the puzzle will automatically fall into place!

## 4) *Signs of a Healthy Coton de Tulear Dog*

The association with pets is seldom built for shorter duration. When you are headed off to purchase your Coton de Tulear, you should be prepared for at least two decades of relationship with its fair share of troubles and memories. This motive is eventually connected with the health of the Coton de Tulear dog. The healthier it is, the longer it will survive.

The quest for healthy pets should begin at the time you purchase it. If your Coton de Tulear dog faces any problems from day one, it is likely to aggravate through its lifetime. While the veterinary doctor and the breeder (those who truly know about the breed) might be able to diagnose a problem beforehand, it is often not as easy for potential buyers like yourself to diagnose problems at such a stage. It is therefore advised for you to book an appointment with a reputed veterinary doctor well in advance so you can get your pet medically evaluated before taking it home.

Despite this, here are some of the factors you should keep in mind before purchasing your Coton de Tulear dog to ensure it is as healthy as possible!

## a. Its Records

Ask the breeder to share your Coton de Tulear dog's heath records with you. This includes detailed information about its vaccinations and all other trips to the veterinary doctor that it might have made. It wouldn't hurt to ask the breeder to get an "all-clear" certificate from a veterinary doctor before you transfer the funds. This will further add towards the credibility of the breeder. Though in case the breeder does provide you with any records, make sure you reach the veterinarian doctor to seek confirmation for the reports.

Much like every other breed, your Coton de Tulear will need to be vaccinated against a host of common dog diseases. However, contrary to other breeds, it shouldn't happen very often. Given the Coton de Tulear dog's small size and tolerance, giving it vaccinations frequently can have adverse reactions.

In fact it has been noted in several accounts that giving a Coton de Tulear multiple vaccinations in one go has created health complications for the puppy. If not identified in a timely manner, these vaccinations can seriously compromise the well being of the Coton de Tulear puppy. In any case, it is advised to seek your veterinary doctor's advice on how to draft up your puppy's schedule of vaccination.

At best, give it one vaccination at a time. If your puppy seems to be reacting badly to it, make a mental note never to repeat the same vaccinations over. Generally, vaccinations are injected more frequently during the early years than when the puppy is older. In case of the Coton de Tulear, the frequency needs to be tuned down further to make sure it doesn't impact your pet negatively.

Your Coton de Tulear will need to be vaccinated against parainfluenza, parovirus, leptospirosis, hepatitis, and distemper. In the beginning, you would need to take your Coton de Tulear to the veterinary doctor every month, that is, the second, third and fourth month without fail. After the fourth month, the frequency of the shots will be reduced to once in a year. Consult your veterinary doctor to find ways to ensure the vaccinations are well dealt with by the Coton de Tulear dog. In case any slightest disturbance occurs, rush to the veterinary doctor immediately to counter the adverse reactions. In the worst case scenarios, negligence may be accompanied by the death of the little one.

## b. Some Physical Indicators

Before you get to the purchase stage, there are a few general signs of good health to be aware of when choosing a healthy puppy from a litter, including the following:

1. **Breathing** – a healthy puppy will breathe quietly, without coughing or sneezing, and there will be no crusting or discharge around their nostrils.
2. **Body** – they will look round and well fed, with an obvious layer of fat over their rib cage.
3. **Coat** – a healthy puppy will have a soft coat with no dandruff, dullness, greasiness or bald spots. In the case of a Coton de Tulear, the cost has to be exceptionally attractive as this is what puts it apart from other breeds.

4. **Energy** – a well rested puppy will be alert and energetic. If it is the other way around, it is most probably a symbol of problem.
5. **Hearing** – a healthy puppy with good hearing should react if you clap your hands behind their head.
6. **Genitals** – a healthy puppy will not have any sort of discharge visible in or around their genital or anal regions.
7. **Mobility** – a healthy puppy will walk and run normally without wobbling, limping or seeming to be weak, stiff or sore.
8. **Vision** – a healthy puppy will have bright, clear eyes without crust or discharge and they should notice if a ball is rolled past them within their field of vision.

If your Coton de Tulear dog seems to be facing certain difficulty in any of these aspects, demand a veterinary inspection before signing the contract.

## 5) *The Registration*

Once you've purchased your Coton de Tulear dog, make sure you get it registered with the American Kennel Club if it is known to be a pedigree. This will ensure a generation of purebreds if you chose to mate your pet. Moreover, the AKC registration will also allow you to participate in a number of dog shows being held around the year in different parts of the world. This will help you get acquainted with other dog owners and to show off your hairy pet to masses.

If you are living in the United Kingdom, make sure you get your pet registered with the Kennel Club of UK. Since the Kennel Club registers both purebreds and mixed breeds, it will not be much of a problem for you to get your pet registered. Play your role in eliminating unhealthy breeding practices. Get your pet registered so that it is eligible to be a part of numerous dog shows happening around the world.

Besides these important facts which compel you to reconsider getting your Coton de Tulear dog registered with the relevant authorities, there are other benefits associated with the registration phase. For instance, if your Coton de Tulear dog manages to escape from its bounds and ends up being captured by the authorities, its registration will keep it alive long enough to allow you the time to come and get it. If your pet isn't registered, it will be given comparatively smaller slice of time to be rescued. If there is no one to own the pet, it will subsequently be put to a never ending sleep. Registration, in effect, ensures longevity for your pet in a legal sense.

Getting your dog registered also saves you from unnecessary penalties. For instance, a registration or license may cost you about $10 to $20 at maximum. However, keeping your dog unregistered can cost you up to $200 in penalty. Decide for yourself – which cost would you rather pay?!

Registration also establishes your ownership over your pet. It is legally and emotionally yours. When it is a well accepted contract between you and your pet, why wouldn't you go just a step further to make sure the world recognizes it too? Dog registration can go a long way in determining how connected you are with your pet.

## 6) Decisions to Buy

There are several other important factors that you need to consider while purchasing the Coton de Tulear dog. Here are a few to get you started with streamlining your options and making the final purchase.

### a. One, Two or More?

How many Coton de Tulear dogs should you buy? Seeing their small size and hyperactive nature, you might be inclined to purchase multiple dogs in one go. Who wouldn't want to be in a house full of small, hairy beings jumping all over the place? This is where you may be headed for serious trouble.

If you have no prior experience handling the Coton de Tulear breed, it is strictly recommended for you to pet one canine at a time. Despite their minute and amiable natures, they may prove to be quite a handful once they are through with the initial adaptation phase. Who would've thought how troublesome the little ones can get!

However, if you are absolutely positive about your decision to purchase multiple Coton de Tulear puppies in one go, feel free to go ahead. If you've transferred the right kind of values and discipline in your pets, it will be extremely rewarding to come home and be greeted by multiple pets at the door!

Beware of competition though. The Coton de Tulear dogs do not like being ignored for some other pet. This is where purchasing multiple puppies in one go may prove to be more fruitful since if a new one if bought after you've pampered the first one, it is bound to feel neglected and hence the number of problems and tantrums it is likely to throw. At the same time, make sure you are not over looking your resource availability – are you ready to take on the responsibility of more than one pet?!

### b.  Male or a Female?

In the big picture, the gender of the Coton de Tulear does not matter. Both are equally affectionate and lovable. Both have roughly the same looks and size. Most of their physical and mental characteristics will match precisely. The only thing where it does matter is when you think about allowing your pet to raise its own family.

With the female dogs in general, the problems pertaining to "coming in heat" and "mating" may be quite painful for your canine friend as well as for you. Same is the case with the male Coton de Tulear though it is a little less daunting since the male ones do not have to face the repercussions of mating. It nevertheless is an issue that demands foresightedness and preplanning to make sure you have the contingency ready by the time the problem is thrust upon you!

Getting your pets spayed and neutered is one way of resolving this emotional conflict though it is quite debatable whether you should indulge in such an activity or not. It most definitely alters the nature of your pet. It was born capable of procreation. Such an act can be considered as a serious violation of animal rights! It is a long winded debate whether one should or should not go for spaying and neutering. You will find more details about this topic in due time. Keep reading to find out all about it.

## c. The Best Age?

The little ones receive their first nutrition from their mothers. Their first values are learnt from their littermates and from their mothers. It is therefore important to allow the Coton de Tulear dog to receive its basic training from its mother before it is separated and put into different homes.

For the first two months, it is strictly recommended not to try separating the litter from its parents. The first eight weeks of its life are crucial in defining its progress through life. Puppies separated before this age might exhibit personality disorders at a later stage. They may also fall ill owing to the separation anxiety as at this tender age, they need their kind the most.

Once the puppies have stabilized, that is, after the first eight weeks of its life, you can try adapting it to the environment. This includes replacing the mother's nutrition with pet food, bringing the pet towards solid foods, incorporating the right amounts of liquids to its diet and so on and so forth. This is the ideal time for adoption!

Besides taking in puppies, you can also go for rescue dogs. They are the ones that come from battered homes and are themselves in a more or less battered state. You can provide shelter to these dogs till the time they meet their natural demise. Often, organizations working with rescue dogs do not charge anything to those caring for the dog.

This, however, translates into more troubles with the pet. They are more likely to have a host of health problems and may also have personality disorders which make taming them a little more difficult. So it is recommended to take in rescue dogs only if you have had prior experience dealing with exceptionally troublesome specimen of their kind!

Keep in mind that at both ages, the requirements of the Coton de Tulear will be very different. Make sure you are able to care for it in the way it deserves. It is the first stepping stone towards a healthy, long term relationship with your Coton de Tulear dog!

# Chapter 8: Preparing to Bring Your Dog Home

If you have shortlisted the breeder, made your choice of puppy and are almost halfway through with the payment and ownership transfer, half of your work is done! The arrival of the new companion is but a matter of days!

While this is undoubtedly an exhilarating experience, think again – have you prepared adequately to accommodate your new friend?

There are a lot of things that need to be done well before you make the move. Make sure you have answered questions like "Where will your pet sleep? What will it eat? How will you keep it occupied?" and so on and so forth!

If you haven't, it is high time you start planning for all these concerns before they hit you on the head in the near future!

Keep in mind that these chores cannot be left until after the dog comes to your home. With the bubbly pet taking up most of your time, you will not have any time to go out shopping!

Furthermore, it is highly unlikely you will be able to go out shopping within two weeks of purchase – the new pet will prove to be quite a handful!

Have your act in order before it puts you to any sort of disadvantage. The next few pages aim to walk you through the basic necessities you need to fulfill in order to assist your pet through its initial transitional phase.

## 1) *Puppy Proofing Your Home*

There are quite a few alterations you will need to make to your house to make it fit for your Coton de Tulear dog. It is all in your best interests and for your pet's well-being.

Puppies, especially those that are teething, like nibbling at things they do not realize might be of importance to you – for instance, your sofa, your chairs, curtains and other accessories around the house.

They also like flexing their claws at things that are resistant like wooden doors.

Here is what you need to do to keep your property and puppy safe from damages.

1. A tall well-rooted fence around your home!
This is because Coton de Tulear dogs have an aptitude of digging in order to build its escape channel. Although it is not likely to do so all the time, it is best to have this contingency in place before your puppy tries to make the escape!

2. Install safety latches in every possible place.
This includes all cabinets and cupboards in the kitchen and elsewhere in the house that are used to stock toxic chemicals like cleaners etc.
You definitely don't want your Coton de Tulear dog to discover these or try experimenting with them.
Also, it is a good idea to install devices on the doors that enables them to close on their own. Keep nurseries, personal rooms and other similar places out of reach of your canine.
If your pet chokes on your child's toy or some other product of similar nature, rest assured the results are least likely to be pleasant!
Keep all medicines, chemicals, cleaners and other potentially hazardous solutions stored behind locked doors at all times!

3. Safe wirings.

Under normal circumstances, leaving a wire or two lying haphazard on the ground is not a big problem; but this is not the case once you have a pet dog in the house.

Inquisitive as they are, they are likely to try playing with the unsheathed wire using their claws. During this little adventure, they might end up exposing the internal copper wirings which may lead to an electric shock.

It is therefore infinitely better to keep these wires stowed away from plain view in the corners of the room.

Also, use a protective covering made from durable plastic to prevent scratches.

Give your pet other safe objects to play with so the wires do not catch its attention!

4. Keep small, potentially dangerous and fragile items away from your pet's reach.

This includes all kinds of decoration pieces made from crystal, glass or other similar material that shatters on impact.

Also, all CDs, DVDs, keys, remotes, kitchen utensils, containers, sharp-edged items, plastic bags and other similar objects that have the tendency to become lethal should be stocked behind locked doors.

Your Coton de Tulear pet does not have as much sense to realize when it is headed for some major trouble. Care for it as you would if it were your offspring!

5. Pet door.

You will need to install one in your main door to allow your dog to move in and out of the house as it pleases.

Make sure it is the right size and does not strangle the canine.

Also, make sure there are no obstructions to its course.

Alternatively, be prepared to see some claw marks on the door if your canine friend finds it closed when and if it needs to go outdoors. This also curtails the call of nature which might be quite messy to clean up.

Invest in a worthwhile pet door to make things easier.

6. The washroom needs dog-proofing as well.

Keep the door closed at all times – use an automatic door lock if necessary.

The flush bowl is an exceptionally attractive place for your pet and it is equally hazardous too! And this does not even cover the dangers of slippery floors!

Best to keep the door of your washroom locked to ban your pet's entry into it.

If you are potty training your pet to use your washroom, make sure you never leave it there unattended until it has been trained properly.

7. Dog-foe plants, edibles and objects to be stored away from reach.

Surprisingly, most dogs don't tolerate chocolates well. So don't leave your wrappers lying around.

Also, if you have any plants that your pet is allergic to, you need to make arrangement to discourage contact. Either change the position of the plant or put it in a place where your pet is not allowed.

8. Use barriers where needed.

This applies equally to indoor uses as well as outdoor uses.

You might want to proof your sofas and cabinets by using a barrier/grill.

Also, if you have an outdoor garden, don't ever leave your dog unattended until and unless you are looking for a major makeover!

Use barriers in front of pools and every other object you don't want your pet to sniff around. It is for its own good!

9. Be careful while using detergents, cleaners and other chemicals.

Their remains are still dangerous for your pet.

Also, garage should be free from chemicals if it is a "can-visit" area for your pet.

Keep your car in regular check to prevent leakages and spills.

Try your level best to keep your pet under supervision at all times. This way you get to control small and innocent mistakes from becoming life-threatening situations.

## *2)  Inspecting the Extent of Puppy Proofing*

Once you are satisfied with your proofing efforts, try looking at the situation from your puppy's point of view. Crouch down on all fours and look around your place from the eye level of a puppy. More often, you will not be able to look into the nook and corners from a higher vantage point as when you are standing upright.

Naturally, this means you might be overlooking a few crucial aspects of puppy proofing the house which might emerge as a major threat later on!

You can turn this into a creative activity for the little ones in your house. Identify all possible hazards and threats and fix them as soon as possible. It is best if your puppy does not have the liberty to explore the hazards before you!

The first few days/weeks are extremely crucial for your pet to settle down. If you successfully make it through these tough days, rest assured there is a rainbow at the other end! It is always better to be safe than sorry. However, in case an accident has taken place or you suspect something is seriously wrong with your pet – probably because it has started acting very weird lately – don't waste a minute and rush it to a veterinary doctor!

A problem nipped in the bud is much better than a situation that needs to be controlled once it has already reached beyond your control! The rest should be fine!

## 3) *Preliminary Shopping List for Your Coton de Tulear*

Be fully prepared to receive your pet in a travel crate – it is the best that will be arranged by most breeders. As the pet is new and possibly bewildered, it is best not to carry it in your arms.

Besides this vital necessity (to make transportation possible), there are a dozen other things you will need to purchase so that your pet can survive a minimum of two weeks in the new home.

If you are planning to take your new pet for shopping even before it has settled, rest assured it is a sure recipe for disaster. Have enough stocks to last you two weeks before you bring the new one home. By this time, your pet will have adjusted to the new owner, new rules and new lifestyle. Hence it will pose fewer challenges while handling.

Here is a list of things you need to purchase – before the new one walks in!

1. Visit to the veterinary. Call in to book your appointment if needed.
It is like a gift from you to your dog – something that it will definitely be thankful for even if it is not able to say it out loud. Have it vaccinated for all major diseases and draft up a schedule for regular checkups. Mark it on your calendar so you don't miss out on it.
Remember, your vet can see beyond the furry shiny coat and hence is in a better state to identify any imminent health problems and diseases.
As in the case of breeder, take your time in locating a certified and genuine veterinary doctor.

2 Pet Food! This includes food, treats and all other form of edibles for your pet.
This is one thing you will need within 24 hours of getting the dog

home. Moreover, this is one thing that is directly related to its health, rationality, irritability and resistance.

Try to get the same stocks of pet food your canine is already accustomed to at the breeder's – so it can feel at home. Be foresighted and get enough food to last you a minimum of two weeks.

3. Food and Water bowls. As much as you would like it, your canine friends cannot feast with you using your kitchen utensils. They need to have their own bowls for food and water.

Make sure you have purchased these beforehand to minimize the stress of finding an alternative impromptu when the need arises. Also, keep in mind that your pet associates these bowls with nutrition and will continue to do so for a long time. So it is a good idea to invest in high-quality and durable bowls.

Have a good look at the breeder's options before making your decision so that your new friend does not feel like a stranger.

4. ID tags, collars and leash. These accessories mark your pet dog and establish your ownership for the world to see.

It is also imperative for you to get these affairs in order well before you get your new companion home. Feeling as a captive being taken away from home, your new pet is likely to make a dash into the unknown whenever it is given the opportunity.

Also, in a foreign neighborhood, chances of it finding its way to your home are next to impossible. So make sure your new friend is fastened adequately to your vehicle to prevent such unfortunate incidences.

Even if it does, the identification documents around its neck will prove to be a life savior – someone else who comes across your dog will be able to return it home if your dog carries its home address!

Keep the Coton de Tulear dog's size, strength and personality traits in mind while shopping for its identification accessories.

5. Dog bed. After a long day of getting accustomed to foreign practices and obeying orders from a relatively unknown master, your dog needs adequate rest so that it wakes up fresh and healthy

the next morning.

A dog bed lined with soft linens and soft cushions work well. If your pet does not sleep well, it will eventually lead it towards bigger health problems.

So make sure you place its bed in a secluded and silent corner of the house. Also, help your pet associate this space with "night" and "sleep" so it is easier to command it to rest.

Rest assured this is not something you can leave on for later – your canine friend needs a good night's sleep every night!

Since the Coton de Tulear dog does not grow too large, you might be able to use the same bed throughout its life. So invest wisely!

6. Dog toys. Dogs don't sleep well with a whole lot of built up energy in their bodies. Assuming you don't have the time or the will to walk your pet every evening/morning in the first few days of association; dog toys are the second best alternative to achieve this motive.

It helps in keeping your pet occupied and entertained (without your active effort). Moreover, dog toys are also an effective way of stimulating the dog's brain and helping it develop its mental capacities.

Use intelligent dog toys and obstacles to help your canine friend develop intellectually and physically – as it would if it were to live in the wild!

7. Travel crate. You won't need it immediately (unless your breeder fails to offer the initial carry crate) but you eventually will.

Imagine the first time you go out shopping after your new pet makes it home. How do you imagine you will carry the fragile being? Carrying it in your arms, though an impressive gesture, will not work well as your pet will feel threatened by the sudden presence of hundreds of other shoppers.

On top of this, there are other places you might need to go to – office, veterinary doctor, your own doctor and others – that will definitely not accommodate an open dog. So it is better to purchase a travel crate well beforehand to keep away from embarrassments.

8. Dog clothes. This becomes exceptionally imperative if you are planning to purchase your Coton de Tulear companion during the winter.

Also, do remember to buy a few warm clothes for your dog if you plan to keep it outdoors – even in the summer. The cold can get to its skin and make it ill before you would realize what has happened.

Keep your defenses up to protect your pet against all odds. Although the Coton de Tulear dog has a heavier coat to battle the winter chill, it nevertheless pays to play your role as the owner.

9. Grooming supplies. Dogs are inquisitive creatures. They have inexplicable interest in finding out what is hidden in the darkest of corners. They can easily be led to places by the smallest of insects. So naturally, they don't last a week without getting dirty. With the Coton de Tulear, the hairy coat poses its own set of challenges as it gets tangled easily. You will need to groom your Coton de Tulear on a daily basis to keep its coat smooth and tangle-free.

Having grooming supplies beforehand therefore is a good idea. Imagine having to go to the supermarket with an unkempt dog that clearly says its master does not care!

Be foresighted enough to prepare for things that are expected to happen. Make sure you search through all alternatives on the market before settling for a few – it helps you get the best possible items!

Also, make sure you have ample supplies to last two weeks. It would typically include a shampoo, scrub, dental hygiene solutions, nail clippers, hair tonic, conditioners, and everything else that you would like to use for your new pet's beauty! The sky is the limit!

Even so, it is recommended not to use a lot of chemicals on your pet as an excess of everything is detrimental!

10. Puppy pads. No one likes to witness a trail of unsightly liquids or solids winded all across the house. The odor makes it even more unbearable. Do yourself a favor and use puppy pads for the first few days – especially if your canine friend is not yet

potty trained.

Train it to use the open outdoors for relieving itself. It will become possible and tolerable over-time!

Once you are out on the shopping spree, you will come across a number of other items that are not on this list but might apparently look useful. Evaluate its utility in the light of your pet before making your purchase.

However, if it seems like an absolute necessity, it is better not to let it be left for a later date.

Admittedly, these accessories summed up with the cost of acquiring a pet (payment to the breeder, registrations etc) can amount to a significant portion of your savings. So you need to be mentally prepared for this kind of expenditure.

It is expected to be an association of a decade or two; so rest assured it will be an ongoing expense rather than just a one-time incident!

Also, keep in mind that most of the items on your shopping list will last quite a few years before they become unusable, broken or "too small" for use (provided you make intelligent decisions in the first place!). So usually the returns on your investment are quite appreciable if you are looking long term.

Having a new companion inevitably calls for a few adjustments. You will need to make quite a few sacrifices to let your new friend settle in. But it will be worth the time and effort!

# Chapter 9: The Initial Days

The initial days will be the most critical ones. If you survive these, you are headed off into a blissful future. Here are a few tips and tricks to prepare you for the first few days and weeks while your Coton de Tulear adjusts with the foreign environment.

## *1) The First Few Days and Weeks*

Before bringing your new companion home, make sure you've put the right barriers in place. Sweep the floors carefully to eliminate all sources of discomfort for the puppy. Also, close the doors to your personal rooms. You puppy does not need to have access to all rooms of the house. Just keep one or two doors open to the rooms that have been puppy-proofed.

Also, make sure you have at least two weeks' puppy supplies readily available with you. Unless you have support at home, you won't be leaving the premises for shopping before the second week. So it is best to have your act in order before the little one walks in.

For the first few weeks, you will have to let your Coton de Tulear get accustomed to the "foreign" environment of your house. It will explore the territories and try to understand what is being expected of it in the given scenario.

It is important for you to be consistent with your puppy's routine – its sleep time, its feeding time, its exercise time and so on and so forth. Inconsistency will give rise to personality disorders and irritability which, in the long run, will impact you negatively!

The first few weeks are ideal for potty training; so invest in your efforts wisely. Let your puppy know where it can relieve itself and where it is considered inappropriate. Kennel training should also be conducted to establish your supremacy over your pet. The first few days and weeks are critical to the long term relationship with your pet – make sure you are investing in its grooming wisely!

Also, never leave your puppy out of supervision. If your puppy is allowed to have its way, it will most surely opt for disaster – for itself as well as for you. Keep a close eye on its activities and curb any evil intentions in the bud. This is important for a healthy relationship later on.

Last but not the least; stay strict but loving with your pet. It needs to know who the boss is but also needs to understand that it is being loved. Don't make it feel too neglected or troubled – it will try to make the run. If it is being pampered too much, it will begin considering itself as the "leader". Establish a balance so the relationship can be carried forth ideally!

## 2) *Setting the Rules*

First and foremost, before you begin training your pet, you need to lay out a few rules in a language that it understands. It may be rules like where to relieve, what to do for play, the rooms which are out of bounds for it and others. You will also need to establish certain hand gestures or words associated with specific actions or meanings.

The first and foremost rule that you need to set is to establish your supremacy over your pet. It needs to understand that you are the only leader in the house. Even with the dominant nature of dogs, your pet needs to understand and register your control. It needs to be subservient to you. It needs to understand that it is in no position to challenge its master. And integration of this value begins when you bring the puppy home.

Never let your puppy lead you into the house. It should always be the one following you around the house. Make sure all human beings are entering the house before the puppy – it tells the dog where it stands in the hierarchy. With the Coton de Tulear, it may not be as easy.

As the Coton de Tulear is a small dog, it becomes a little difficult to resist its sprightly behavior. Nevertheless, if you are looking for a well behaved puppy, you will need to harden yourself and treat it as you would treat a bigger dog. All dogs essentially have the same nature – they need to be treated alike in order to keep them disciplined.

Besides this, keep the no-puppy zones in your house locked at all times. If you see your puppy trying to break in, let it know this behavior is undesirable. Penalize it if necessary – it will not try to transgress limits once it understands.

Let your puppy know where it is supposed to sleep, eat or drink. Also, build a schedule for its activities – when it is supposed to feast or sleep. Administer these values so the Coton de Tulear is less challenging when it matures.

## 3) *Common Mistakes to Avoid*

There are several mistakes you are most likely to commit while caring for your pet. You won't indulge in these mistakes deliberately – it rather happens unintentionally. Nevertheless, it can have long lasting impact on your puppy's grooming and discipline.

Here are few of the most common mistakes people are known to make with their pets:

1. Let the puppy sleep in bed with you. It is a sure recipe for disaster. You let the puppy believe it is equivalent – if not superior – to you.
2. Free feeding. That is another way of reinforcing its dominating characteristics. It should be made to follow a feeding schedule.

3. Playing too hard or too long. It will begin reflecting on the puppy's health. Let it rest adequately.
4. Reinforcing wrong habits. You need to define a line between what is cute and acceptable and what is cute but not acceptable. With small sized dogs, it is a big problem. They look cute if they jump into your lap, but a bigger dog doesn't. So you discipline both dogs differently which may give rise to the small dog syndrome. Make sure you are not reinforcing any unlikeable behaviors in your pet. Evaluate your relationship with your pet critically.
5. Grooming. Get your pet accustomed to grooming procedures. If it becomes averse to frequent grooming, well then best of luck with the Coton de Tulear dog's tangled hairs!

## 4) Ways to Bond With Your Coton de Tulear

The Coton de Tulear is a sprightly dog with a lot of energy and love to share. You will begin bonding with your Coton de Tulear puppy from the very first moment you bring them home from the breeders.

This is the time when your puppy will be the most upset and nervous, as they will no longer have the guidance, warmth and comfort of their mother or their other littermates, and you will need to take on the role of being your new puppy's center of attention.

Be patient, kind and gentle with them as they are learning you are now their new center of the universe.

Your daily interaction with your puppy during play sessions and especially your disciplined exercises, including going for walks on leash, and teaching commands and tricks, will all be wonderful bonding opportunities. Do not make the mistake of thinking that *"bonding"* with your new puppy can only happen if you are playing or cuddling together, because the very best bonding happens when you are kindly teaching rules and boundaries, and this intelligent puppy will be most eager to learn.

**What Does the Wag Mean?**

It can be a mistake to automatically assume that if a dog is wagging their tail that they are happy and friendly.

When determining a dog's true intent or demeanor, you need to take into consideration the entire dog because it is entirely possible that a dog can be wagging its tail just before it decides to take an aggressive lunge toward you.

More important in determining the emotional state of a dog is the height or positioning of their tail.

For instance, a tail that is held parallel to the dog's back usually suggests that the dog is feeling relaxed, whereas, if the tail is held stiffly vertical, this usually means that the dog is feeling aggressive or dominant.

A tail held much lower can mean that the dog is feeling stressed, afraid, submissive or unwell and if the tail is tucked underneath the dog's body, this is most often a sign that the dog is feeling fearful and threatened by another dog or person.

Paying attention to your dog's tail can help you to know when you need to step in and make some space between your dog and another more dominant dog.

Of course, different breeds naturally carry their tails at different heights, so you will need to take this into consideration when studying your dog's tail so that you get used to their particular signals.

As well, the speed the tail is moving will also give you an idea of the mental state of the dog because the speed of the wag usually indicates how excited a dog may be.

For instance, a slow, slightly swinging wag can often mean that the dog is tentative about greeting another dog, and this is more of a questioning type of wag, whereas a fast moving tail held high can mean that a dog is about to challenge or threaten another less dominant dog.

Interestingly, two veterinarians at the University of Bari and a neuroscientist at the University of Trieste, in Italy, published a paper in which their research outlined that dogs' tails wagged more to their right side when they had positive feelings about a person or situation, and more to the left side when they were feeling negative.

While certainly a dog's tail can help us humans to understand how our dogs might be feeling, there are many other factors to take into consideration when determining your dog's state of mind.

# Chapter 10: Common Health Problems

I will talk more about medical concerns later in this book The Coton de Tulear in general is a fairly healthy breed. There aren't any health problems associated with this breed. This may be attributed to the fact that extra emphasis is being placed to keep the gene pool clean and healthy. It takes a lot of scrutiny and regularization to get the puppy registered as a Coton de Tulear.

However, as with most breeds, there may be instances when the Coton de Tulear is known to get affected by cherry-eye, progressive retinal atrophy, patellar luxation, canine hip dysplasia, Legg Calve Perthes disease and a few others medical conditions.

In some cases, these problems cannot be diagnosed beforehand or eliminated from the gene pool. These problems commonly include progressive blindness (also known as progressive retinal atrophy) and cerebellar ataxia. There may be ways to slow down the degenerative process but it does happen in its due course of time.

## 1) *Early Diagnosis*

Before you reach out to pick up your puppy from the breeder's, make sure you look for the parent's DNA reports. They should be tested for Canine multi-focal retinopathy, von Willebrands disease Type 1 and Neonatal ataxia. This helps diagnose problems in the early stages so that your puppy can grow old with you in health and wellness.

Besides this, hip and elbow dysplasia, cardiac problems, neuro-diseases and other similar non-life-threatening issues can be identified in time through regular consultation with the veterinary doctor. Usually, these problems begin by emitting extremely subliminal signs. They are often misinterpreted by the human eye but the veterinary doctor is trained to understand these fine lines correctly. They can therefore identify and nip the problem in the bud while you consider the signs to be normal or natural to its maturity.

## 2) Shots, Vaccinations and Regular Check-Ups

Your pet – irrespective of which species or breed it is – will need to be vaccinated against a wide range of diseases. This is done to ensure longevity and better immune system development for your pet. However, in case of the Coton de Tulear, you are encouraged to vaccinate it against one disease at a time. Avoid using 5-in-one immune boosters as they may backfire.

There have been instances when certain Coton de Tulear dogs exhibited allergic reactions to vaccination shots. Don't inject vaccinations unnecessarily. In fact, your Coton de Tulear is strong enough to tolerate a number of minor health problems naturally.

Discuss in detail with your veterinary doctor about how to take care of your Coton de Tulear dog. Also, express your concerns over the vaccination schedule if any. Make sure you and your veterinary doctor are on the same page with respect to the Coton de Tulear dog.

Don't forget to take your pet in for regular check-ups. Once your pet is through with its initial vaccinations and shots, make sure you are still paying a visit to the veterinary doctor every month or two. This will help your vet diagnose problems in the early stages and treat accordingly.

Your Coton de Tulear needs to be vaccinated every month for the first four months of its life. Then on, the frequency is reduced to once a year. Make sure you are not missing out on these appointments. Your pet's health and well being is your responsibility, so make sure you are proving to be the right owner for your canine companion!

# Chapter 11: Caring for Your Coton de Tulear

So far you've been exposed to the idea of getting a Coton de Tulear dog, purchasing and bringing it home, keeping it healthy and being a responsible owner. However, this is where the real challenge begins. This sections talks about how you will be required to care for your Coton de Tulear dog – from the very basics to the advanced maintenance regimes. Read through this section carefully to understand how best to care for your puppy.

## *1) Its Grooming Concerns*

The first thing any one sees about your pet is how well it is kept. They don't groom themselves; you need to be making an active effort to keep your Coton de Tulear presentable at all times. Here are a few grooming tips that you need to be careful about.

### a. Its Coat

The Coton de Tulear has a long coat that is made up of distinctive strands of hair. It is relatively a non-shedding breed – an occasional hair or two on your couch should not raise an alarm for you. The hair keeps the Coton de Tulear warm during the winter months and provides an additional cushion against injuries. However, you might need to trim down the hair at times to make sure it does not obstruct the Coton de Tulear dog's vision or limit its capabilities in any way. The rest should be fine.

### b. Its Nails

Allowing your Coton de Tulear to have long, untrimmed nails can result in various health hazards including infections or an irregular and uncomfortable gait that can result in damage to their skeleton.

Although most dogs do not particular enjoy the process of having their nails trimmed, and most humans find the exercise to be a little scary, regular nail trimming is a very important grooming practice that should never be overlooked.

In order to keep your adult Coton de Tulear dog's toenails in good condition and the proper length, you will need to purchase a plier type nail trimmer at a pet store and learn how to correctly use it.

When your Coton de Tulear is a small puppy, it will be best to trim their nails with a pair of nail scissors, which you can purchase at any pet store, that are smaller and easier to use on puppy nails. All you need to do is snip off the curved tip of each nail.

Further, if you want your dog's nails to be smooth, without the sharp edges clipping alone can create, you will also want to invest in a toenail file or a special, slow speed, rotary Dremel™ trimmer, equipped with a sanding disk, which is designed especially for dog nails. Some dogs will prefer the rotary trimmer to the squeezing sensation of the nail clipper and when you keep your dog's nails regularly trimmed, the Dremel™ may be the only tool you will ever need.

### c.  Dental Hygiene

Yes, your dog needs regular brushing as well. Bad breath and inadequate dental hygiene can eventually lead to bigger problems – including upset stomach and halitosis. Make sure you brush your pet's teeth every day (or every few days)!

You can use commercially produced products or use homemade ones by combining baking soda with water. Use soft nylon cloth or commercial toothbrushes to clean its teeth. Don't agitate your pet as its teeth are the last place you want to be near to while it is angry!

Inability to do so can lead your Coton de Tulear dog towards gum diseases that can aggravate into teeth-loss. Keep your dog's smile healthy – brush its teeth and gums regularly.

Have its teeth and gums regularly inspected by the veterinary doctor. This will help in diagnosing a problem at the earliest. Consequently, it will be easier to devise a plan of action to overcome this problem in a timely manner.

### d. Its Ears

Have your Coton de Tulear dog checked regularly for ear infections. Ear cropping does not prevent ear infections. This becomes more important once your Coton de Tulear has had its periodic bath.

You can find a number of chemical solutions in the market to clean your pet's ears. Make sure you've consulted the veterinarian before using any.

Also, seek advice from your veterinary doctor to find out how best to clean your canine's ears. Too much debris can build up into a major health problem. Most evidently though, too much debris can lead to loss of hearing which might be misinterpreted as lack of obedience.

Do yourself and your Coton de Tulear dog a favor; clean its ears regularly. So you can nurture a well-rounded relationship with your pet!

### e. Its Eyes

Every dog should have their eyes regularly wiped with a warm, damp cloth to remove build up of daily secretions in the corners of the eyes that can be unattractive and uncomfortable for the dog as the hair becomes glued together.

If this build up is not removed every day, it can quickly become a cause of bacterial yeast growth that can lead to eye infections.

When you take a moment every day to gently wipe your dog's eyes with a warm, moist cloth, you will help to keep your dog's eyes comfortable and infection free.

## f. Bathing

**Step One**: Before you get your Coton de Tulear anywhere near the water, it's important to make sure that you brush out any debris, or dead hair from their coat before you begin the bathing process.

As well, removing any debris from your dog's coat beforehand will make the entire process easier on you, your dog, and your drains, which will become clogged with dead hair if you don't remove it beforehand.

**Step Two**: If your Coton de Tulear has a longer coat, the process will be much easier if you first spray the coat with a light mist of leave-in conditioner before brushing. This will also help to protect the hair strands against breakage.

**Step Three**: Whether you're bathing your Coton de Tulear in your laundry tub, bathtub or sink, you will always want to first lay down a rubber bath mat to provide a more secure footing for your dog and to prevent your tub or sink from being scratched.

**Step Four**: Have everything you need for the bath (shampoo, conditioner, sponge, towels) right next to the sink or tub, so you don't have to go searching once your dog is already in the water.

Place cotton balls in your Coton de Tulear dog's ear canals to prevent accidental splashes from entering the ear canal that could later cause an ear infection.

**Step Five**: Fill the tub or sink with four to six inches of lukewarm water (not too hot as dogs are more sensitive to hot water than us humans) and put your Coton de Tulear dog in the water. Completely wet your dog's coat right down to the skin by using a detachable showerhead. If you don't have a spray attachment, a cup or pitcher will work just as well.

**Step Six**: Apply shampoo as indicated on the bottle instructions by beginning at the head and working your way down the back. Be careful not to get shampoo in the eyes, nose, mouth or ears. Comb the shampoo lather through your dog's hair with your fingers, making sure you don't miss the areas under the legs and tail.

**Step Seven**: After allowing the shampoo to remain in your dog's coat for a couple of minutes, thoroughly rinse the Coton de Tulear dog's coat, right down to the skin with clean, lukewarm water using the spray attachment, cup or pitcher. Comb through your dog's coat with your fingers to make sure all shampoo residues has been completely rinsed away.

Any shampoo remaining in a dog's coat will lead to irritation and itching. Once you've rinsed, take the time to rinse again, especially in the armpits and underneath the tail area.

Use your hands to gently squeeze all excess water from your dog's coat.

**Step Eight**: Apply conditioner as indicated on the bottle instructions and work the conditioner throughout your dog's coat. Leave the conditioner in your dog's coat for two minutes and then thoroughly rinse again with warm water, unless the conditioner you are using is a *"leave-in"*, no-rinse formula.

The best conditioner for a Coton de Tulear will contain mink oil, which adds a gloss to deepen and enrich the natural color of the coat.

It is also a good idea to choose a brand of conditioner that contains sunscreen to help protect from ultraviolet radiation when your dog is outside on sunny days.

Applying a good conditioner containing protein to your Coton de Tulear dog's coat after bathing will help to rebuild, restructure and protect the coat by bonding to the shaft of each individual hair.

Pull the plug on your sink or tub and let the water drain away as you use your hands to squeeze excess water from your Coton de Tulear dog's legs and feet.

**Step Nine**: Immediately out of the water, wrap your Coton de Tulear in dry towels so they don't get cold and use the towels to gently squeeze out extra water before you allow them to shake and spray water everywhere.

If your dog has longer hair, do not rub their coat with the towels, as this will create tangles and breakage in the longer hair.

Dry your Coton de Tulear right away with your hand held hairdryer and be careful not to let the hot air get too close to their skin.

If your Coton de Tulear dog's hair is longer, blow the hair in the direction of growth to help prevent breakage and if the hair is short, you can use your hand or a soft brush or comb to lift and fluff the coat to help it dry more quickly.

Place your hand between the hairdryer and your Coton de Tulear dog's hair so that they will never get a direct blast of hot air and never blow air directly into their face or ears.

Don't forget to remove the cotton balls from their ears.

## g. Brushing and Combing

Your Coton de Tulear will have long hairs that are prone to get tangled unless they are cut short. Its hair is also one of the most attractive features particular to this breed. In order to get the best of everything, you will need to brush its coat on a daily basis –

preferably multiple times during the day – to keep it free from tangles.

Use a soft and organic brush to straighten its hair. Also, always brush its hair in one direction making sure it is aligned properly with the direction of growth. Combing the hairs in any other direction will put unnecessary strain on the hair and cause breakage.

Brushing the hair multiple times during the day will ensure there are no unnecessary tangles forming in the canine's coat. Brushing and combing is one way to express your love for your canine and will therefore help in bonding. Make sure you are spending sufficient time at the task.

Also, don't brush the hair on the surface. Make sure you are stimulating the skin as well through the brushing process. This will not only improve the blood circulation towards the hairs and skin but also improve the quality of hair.

The key to grooming your Coton de Tulear is to prevent its hair from tangling into knots. These notorious knots can become a challenge to untangle – in worst case scenario; you might need to remove the knots by cutting off the hair. Brush regularly and bathe it periodically. If your Coton de Tulear looks presentable, you've done a commendable job of caring for it!

## 2) *Feeding Concerns*

The next important thing you need to be aware about is the feeding concerns your pet has. Here is a little insight into the Coton de Tulear dog's eating patterns.

### a. Feeding Young Coton de Tulear Dogs

For growing puppies, a general feeding rule of thumb is to feed 10% of the puppy's present body weight or between 2% and 3% of their projected adult weight each day.

Keep in mind that high energy puppies will require extra protein to help them grow and develop into healthy adult dogs, especially during their first two years of life.

There are now many foods on the market that are formulated for all stages of a dog's life (including the puppy stage), so whether you choose one of these foods or a food specially formulated for puppies, they will need to be fed smaller meals more frequently throughout the day (3 or 4 times), until they are at least one year of age.

Choose quality sources of meat protein for healthy puppies and dogs, including beef, buffalo, chicken, duck, fish, hare, lamb, ostrich, pork, rabbit, turkey, venison, or any other source of wild meaty protein.

## b. Feeding Adult Coton de Tulear Dogs

An adult dog will generally need to be fed between 2% and 3% of their body weight each day. Read the labels and avoid foods that contain a high amount of grains and other fillers. Choose foods that list high quality meat protein as the main ingredient.

## c. Frequency of Feeding

How frequently you need to feed your Coton de Tulear largely depends on its physical characteristics. For instance, some Coton de Tulear dogs like to consume several small servings during the day, a few eat well in the evening while a few might work well with a twice-a-day regime. By and large, you will need to contemplate the type of Coton de Tulear you've ended up with.

Ideally, during the early months, it is recommended to feed your Coton de Tulear multiple servings during the day – about four small servings throughout the day. Once your Coton de Tulear hits the six-month mark, you can try reducing the frequency to thrice or twice per day.

Keep in mind that your Coton de Tulear should not have the liberty to feed as and when it wills. Designate a specific time frame in which the Coton de Tulear is allowed to feast – this time frame should range between a few hours at stretch. Let's say you put out a bowl in the morning; make sure you've removed it by early afternoon. Likewise, when you put out its evening bowl, make sure you remove it before night falls. The Coton de Tulear will be free to feed as and when it wills during the specified time frame but not otherwise!

For Coton de Tulear dogs, grazing is a common habit. You will therefore need to leave its food out for several hours at a stretch in order to get your pet to eat something. Make sure your pet is not going to bed on an empty stomach. If your pet seems to have any particular food preferences, respect these. Food defines your pet's health in the short as well as the long run – make sure it isn't being compromised.

## d. Treats

Since the creation of the first dog treat over 150 years ago the myriad of choices available on every pet store, feed store and grocery store shelf almost outnumbers those looking forward to eating them.

Today's treats are not just for making us guilty humans feel better because it makes us happy to give our fur friends something they really enjoy because today's treats are also designed to actually improve our dog's health.

Some of us humans treat our dogs, just because, others use treats for training purposes, others for health, while still others treat for a combination of reasons.

Whatever reason you choose to give treats to your Coton de Tulear, keep in mind that if we treat our dogs too often throughout the day, we may create a picky eater who will no longer want to eat their regular meals.

As well, if the treats we are giving are high calorie, we may be putting our dog's health in jeopardy by allowing them to become overweight.

### e. Healthy Treats

Here are a few healthy treats that you can treat your Coton de Tulear with!

### Hard Treats

There are so many choices of hard or crunchy treats available that come in many varieties of shapes, sizes and flavors, that you may have a difficult time choosing.

If your Coton de Tulear will eat them, hard treats will help to keep their teeth cleaner.

Whatever you do choose, be certain to read the labels and make sure that the ingredients are high quality and appropriately sized for your Coton de Tulear friend.

### Soft Treats

Soft, chewy treats are also available in a wide variety of flavors, shapes and sizes for all the different needs of our fur friends and are often used for training purposes as they have a stronger smell.

### Dental Treats

Dental treats or chews are designed with the specific purpose of helping your Coton de Tulear to maintain healthy teeth and gums.

They usually require intensive chewing and are often shaped with high ridges and bumps to exercise the jaw and massage gums while removing plaque build-up near the gum line.

**Freeze-Dried and Jerky Treats**

Freeze-dried and jerky treats offer a tasty morsel most dogs find irresistible as they are usually made of simple, meaty ingredients, such as liver, poultry and seafood.

These treats are usually lightweight and easy to carry around, which means they can also be great as training treats.

**Human Food Treats**

You will want to be very careful when feeding human foods to dogs as treats, because many of our foods contain additives and ingredients that could be toxic and harmful.

Be certain to choose simple, fresh foods with minimal or no processing, such as lean meat, poultry or seafood, and even if your Coton de Tulear will eat anything put in front of them, be aware that many common human foods, such as grapes, raisins, onions and chocolate are poisonous to dogs.

**Training Treats**

While any sort of treat can be used as an extra incentive during training sessions, soft treats are often used for training purposes because of their stronger smell and smaller sizes.

Yes, we humans love to treat our dogs, whether for helping to teach the new puppy to go pee outside, teaching the adolescent dog new commands, for trick training, for general good behavior, or for no reason at all, other than that they just gave us the *"look"*.

Generally, the treats you feed your dog should not make up more than approximately 10% of their daily food intake, so make sure the treats you choose are high quality, so that you can help to keep your Coton de Tulear both happy and healthy.

## f. Harmful Treats

Not all treats are healthy for your puppy's consumption. Here are a few harmful treats you should be aware of. Eliminate these from your shopping list to ensure a long and happy life for your Coton de Tulear puppy!

## Rawhide

Rawhide is soaked in an ash/lye solution to remove every particle of meat, fat and hair and then further soaked in bleach to remove remaining traces of the ash/lye solution. Now that the product is no longer food, it no longer has to comply with food regulations.

While the hide is still wet it is shaped into rawhide chews, and upon drying it shrinks to approximately 1/4 of its original size.

Further, arsenic based products are often used as preservatives, and antibiotics and insecticides are added to kill bacteria that also fight against good bacteria in your dog's intestines.

The collagen fibers in the rawhide make it very tough and long lasting which makes this chew a popular choice for humans to give to their dogs because it satisfies the dog's natural urge to chew while providing many hours of quiet entertainment.

Sadly, when a dog chews a rawhide treat, they ingest many harsh chemicals and when your dog swallows a piece of rawhide, that piece can swell up to four times its normal size inside your dog's stomach, which can cause anything from mild to severe gastric blockages that could become life threatening and require surgery.

## Pig Ears

These treats are actually the ears of pigs, and while most dogs will eagerly devour them, they are extremely high in fat, which can cause stomach upsets, vomiting and diarrhea for many dogs.

Pig ears are often processed and preserved with unhealthy chemicals that discerning dog guardians will not want to feed their dogs.

As well, the ears are often quite thin and crispy and when the dog chews them pieces can break off, like chips, and can easily become stuck in a dog's throat.

While pig ears are generally not considered to be a healthy treat choice for any dog, they should be especially avoided for any dog that may be at risk of being overweight.

**Hoof Treats**

Many humans give cow, horse and pig hooves to their dogs as treats because they consider them to be *"natural"*.

The truth is that after processing these *"treats"* they retain little, if any, of their *"natural"* qualities.

Hoof treats are processed with harsh preservatives, including insecticides, lead, bleach, arsenic based products, and antibiotics to kill bacteria, that can also harm the good bacteria in your dog's intestines, and if all bacteria is not killed in these meat based products before feeding them to your dog, they could also suffer from Salmonella poisoning.

Hooves can also cause chipping or breaking of your dog's teeth as well as perforation or blockages in your dog's intestines.

**g. Choosing the Right Food**

In order to choose the right food for your Coton de Tulear, first, it's important to understand a little bit about canine physiology and what Mother Nature intended when she created our fur friends.

More than 230 years ago, in 1785, the English Sportman's dictionary described the best diet for a dog's health in an article entitled *"Dog"*.

This article indicated that the best food for a dog was something called *"Greaves"*, described as *"the sediment of melted tallow. It is made into cakes for dogs' food. In Scotland and parts of the US it is called cracklings."*

Out of the meager beginning of the first commercially made dog food has sprung a massively lucrative and vastly confusing industry that has only recently begun to evolve beyond those early days of feeding our dogs the dregs of human leftovers because it was cheap and convenient for us humans.

Even today, the majority of dog food choices have far more to do with being convenient for humans to store and serve than it does with being a diet truly designed to be a nutritionally balanced, healthy food choice for a canine.

The dog food industry is big business and as such, because there are now almost limitless choices, there is much confusion and endless debate when it comes to answering the question, *"What is the best food for my dog?"*

Educating yourself, by talking to experts and reading everything you can find on the subject, plus taking into consideration several relevant factors, will help to answer the dog food question for you and your dog.

For instance, where you live may dictate what sorts of foods you have access to. Other factors to consider will include the particular requirements of your dog, such as their age, energy and activity levels.

Next will be expense, time and quality. While we all want to give our dogs the best food possible, many humans lead very busy lives and cannot, for instance, prepare their own dog food, but still want to feed a high quality diet that fits within their budget.

However, perhaps most important when choosing an appropriate diet for our dogs, is learning to be more observant of Mother Nature's design and taking a closer look at our dog's teeth, jaws and digestive tract. While humans are herbivores who derive energy from eating plants, our canine companions are carnivores, which means that they derive their energy and nutrient requirements from eating a diet consisting mainly or exclusively of the flesh of animal tissues (in other words, meat).

**The Canine Teeth**

The first part of your dog you will want to take a good look at when considering what to feed will be their teeth. Unlike humans, who are equipped with wide, flat molars for grinding grains, vegetables and other plant-based materials, canine teeth are all pointed because they are designed to rip, shred and tear into animal meat and bone.

**The Canine Jaw**

Another obvious consideration when choosing an appropriate food source for our fur friends is the fact that every canine is born equipped with powerful jaws and neck muscles for the specific purpose of being able to pull down and tear apart their hunted prey. The structure of the jaw of every canine is such that it opens widely to hold large pieces of meat and bone, while the actual mechanics of a dog's jaw permits only vertical (up and down) movement that is designed for crushing.

**The Canine Digestive Tract**

A dog's digestive tract is short and simple and designed to move their natural choice of food (hide, meat and bone) quickly through their systems.

Vegetables and plant matter require more time to break down in the gastrointestinal tract, which in turn, requires a more complex digestive system than the canine body is equipped with.

The canine digestive system is simply unable to break down vegetable matter, which is why whole vegetables look pretty much the same going into your dog as they do coming out the other end.

Given the choice, most dogs would never choose to eat plants or vegetables and fruits over meat; however, we humans continue to feed them a kibble based diet that contains high amounts of vegetables, fruits and grains and low amounts of meat.

Plus, in order to get our dogs to eat fruits, vegetables and grains we usually have to flavor the food with meat or meat by-products.

How much healthier and long lived might our beloved fur friends will be if, instead of largely ignoring nature's design for our canine companions, we chose to feed them whole, unprocessed, species-appropriate food?

With many hundreds of dog food brands to choose from, it's no wonder we humans are confused about what to feed our dogs to help them live long and healthy lives.

Following are some suggestions and questions that may help you choose a dog food company that you can feel comfortable with:

- How long have they have been in business?
- Is dog food their main industry?
- Are they dedicated to their brand?
- Are they easily accessible?
- Do they honestly answer your questions?
- Do they have a good Company Safety Standard?
- Do they set higher standards?
- Read the ingredients - where did they come from?
- Are the ingredients something you would eat?

- Are the ingredients farmed locally?
- Was it cooked using standards you would trust?
- Is the company certified under human food or organic guidelines?

Whatever you decide to feed your Coton de Tulear dog, keep in mind that, just as too much wheat, other grains and other fillers in our human diet is having detrimental effects on our human health, the same can be very true for our best fur friends.

Our dogs are also suffering from many of the same life threatening diseases that are rampant in our human society (heart disease, cancer) as a direct result of consuming a diet high in genetically altered, impure, processed and packaged foods.

## h. The Raw Diet

While some of us believe we are killing ourselves as well as our dogs with processed foods, others believe that there are dangers in feeding raw foods.

Those who are raw feeding advocates believe that the ideal diet for their dog is one which would be very similar to what a dog living in the wild would have access to hunting or foraging, and these canine guardians are often opposed to feeding their dog any sort of commercially manufactured pet foods, because they consider them to be poor substitutes.

On the other hand, those opposed to feeding their dogs a raw or biologically appropriate raw food diet, believe that the risks associated with food-borne illnesses during the handling and feeding of raw meats outweigh the purported benefits.

Interestingly, even though the United States Food and Drug Administration (FDA) states that they do not advocate a raw diet for dogs, they do advise for those who wish to take this route, that following basic hygiene guidelines for handling raw meat can minimize any associated risks.

Further, high pressure pasteurization (HPP), which is high pressure, water based technology for killing bacteria, is USDA-approved for use on organic and natural food products, and is being utilized by many commercial raw pet food manufacturers.

Interestingly, raw meats purchased at your local grocery store contain a much higher level of acceptable bacteria than raw food produced for dogs because the meat purchased for human consumption is supposed to be cooked, which will kill any bacteria that might be present.

This means that canine guardians feeding their dogs a raw food diet can be quite certain that commercially prepared raw foods sold in pet stores will be safer than raw meats purchased in grocery stores.

Many guardians of high energy, working breed dogs will agree that their dogs thrive on a raw or BARF (Biologically Appropriate Raw Food) diet and strongly believe that the potential benefits of feeding a raw dog food diet are many, including:

- healthy, shiny coats
- decreased shedding
- fewer allergy problems
- healthier skin
- cleaner teeth
- fresher breath
- higher energy levels
- improved digestion
- smaller stools
- strengthened immune system
- increased mobility in arthritic pets
- increase or improvement in overall health

All dogs, of every size, whether working breed or companion dogs are amazing athletes in their own right, therefore every dog deserves to be fed the best food available.

A raw diet is a direct evolution of what dogs ate before they became our domesticated pets and we turned toward commercially prepared, easy to serve dry dog food that required no special storage or preparation.

The BARF diet is all about feeding our dogs what they are designed to eat by returning them to their wild, evolutionary diet.

### i.   The Dehydrated Diet

Dehydrated dog food comes in both raw meat and cooked meat forms and these foods are usually air dried to reduce moisture to the level where bacterial growth is inhibited.

The appearance of de-hydrated dog food is very similar to dry kibble and the typical feeding methods include adding warm water before serving, which makes this type of diet both healthy for our dogs and convenient for us to serve.

Dehydrated recipes are made from minimally processed fresh whole foods to create a healthy and nutritionally balanced meal that will meet or exceed the dietary requirements of a healthy canine. Dehydrating removes only the moisture from the fresh ingredients, which usually means that because the food has not already been cooked at a high temperature, more of the overall nutrition is retained.

A de-hydrated diet is a convenient way to feed your dog a nutritious diet because all you have to do is add warm water, and wait five minutes while the food re-hydrates so your Coton de Tulear can enjoy a warm meal.

## j.  The Kibble Diet

While many canine guardians are starting to take a closer look at the food choices they are making for their furry companions, there is no mistaking that the convenience and relative economy of dry dog food kibble, that had its beginnings in the 1940's, continues to be the most popular pet food choice for most dog friendly humans.

Some 75 years later, the massive pet food industry offers up a confusingly large number of choices with hundreds of different manufacturers and brand names lining the shelves of veterinarian offices, grocery stores and pet food aisles.

While feeding a high quality bagged kibble diet that has been flavored to appeal to dogs and supplemented with vegetables and fruits to appeal to humans, may keep most every Coton de Tulear companion happy and relatively healthy, you will ultimately need to decide whether this is the best diet for them.

## k.  The Right Feeding Bowl

Following is a brief description of the different categories and types of dog bowls that would be appropriate choices for your Coton de Tulear's particular needs.

**Automatic Watering Bowls**: are standard dog bowls (often made out of plastic) that are attached to a reservoir container, which is designed to keep water constantly available to your dog as long as there is water remaining in the storage compartment.

**Ceramic/Stoneware Bowls**: an excellent choice for those who like options in personality, color and shape.

**Elevated Bowls**: raised dining table dog bowls are a tidy and classy choice that will make your dog's dinner time a more comfortable experience while getting the bowls off the floor.

**No Skid Bowls**: are for dogs that push their bowls across the floor when eating. A non-skid dog bowl will help keep the feed bowl where you put it.

**No Tip Bowls**: are designed to prevent the messy type of doggy eater from flipping over their dinner or water bowls.

**Stainless Steel Bowls**: are as close to indestructible as a bowl can be, plus they are sanitary, easy to clean and water stays cooler for a longer period of time in a stainless bowl.

**Wooden Bowls**: for those humans concerned about stylish home decor, wooden dog bowl dining stations are beautiful pieces of furniture unto themselves that can enhance your home decor.

**Travel Bowls**: are convenient, practical and handy additions for every canine travel kit.

Consider a space saving, collapsible dog bowl, made out of hygienic, renewable bamboo that comes in fun colors and different sizes, making it perfect for every travel bowl needs.

If you would like to learn more about all the many dog bowl choices available, visit DogBowlForYourDog.com, which is a comprehensive, one-stop website dedicated to explaining the ins and outs of every food bowl imaginable and helping you find the perfect bowl for all your Coton de Tulear's needs.

## 3) *Accommodating the Coton de Tulear*

It is never easy to take up a companion; especially because every entity is unique. Different species have different needs, which make it challenging to adjust. Your Coton de Tulear is no exception to this.

There are certain specific needs of the Coton de Tulear dog that you need to keep in mind at all times. These do not only affect the health and well being of your pet but also determines how quickly your pet adjusts with you.

Here are some of the aspects of its accommodation phase that you need to keep in mind while bringing your newfound companion home.

### a. Its Sleep Area

Generally, all dogs like having a dedicated space for their sleep. This means a separate room or a specific corner of your house. Also, it is best if it is a secluded and silent spot. If you design the Coton de Tulear dog's sleep area in the middle of commotion, rest assured it will not be able to sleep. Instead, it will jump up to the occasion and start playing around with you every time you pass by its sleep area.

Keep in mind never to let the Coton de Tulear dog sleep with you in your bed. Admittedly, being a small dog, your Coton de Tulear will not take up a lot of space on your bed and will therefore adjust in easily. However, by doing so, you will end up reinforcing negative habits and traits in your Coton de Tulear dog. It will begin considering itself to be the leader of the "pack" and will therefore become a challenge to maintain. Define the boundaries for your pet while you still can.

### b. Exercise Area

Coton de Tulear is a small dog and therefore will not have a lot of built up energy resource that needs to be expended. A daily walk around a park or in the streets suffices to provide for its exercise needs. However, make sure you are not carrying it in your arms or letting it trot by your side without a leash. The former case kills the purpose of the walk altogether and the latter one accentuates the probability of an escape.

Familiarize your Coton de Tulear with the neighborhood during the first few weeks. This will ensure your Coton de Tulear is able to find its way back if and when it makes a dash into the wilderness. However, never let it off the leash. The cute and amiable appearance of the Coton de Tulear can be dissolved in minutes if the dog feels threatened.

Take it for a walk on a daily basis and make sure you include a weekly or monthly hike in its exercise routine as well. This will not only keep your puppy fit and healthy but also work just the same for you!

## c. Play Area

This is the area where your puppy will spend most of its time getting entertained by mindless activities. It is also the place where you will most probably be leaving the puppy without active supervision. It is therefore a natural instinct to puppy-proof this area to the best of your capacity.

Clear the room of all "human" furniture. It'll be a good idea to install a fixed carpet in this room to provide greater stability for its feet. Add in a few toys to this room that your pet likes and is unlikely to choke on and you are done! If there are any windows or doors in the room, make sure you install adequate barriers to keep the puppy in as once it gets bored, it will try to get out and explore "the world beyond"!

Mazes and obstacle courses can stimulate your pet's mind and facilitate its physical as well as mental development. Make sure you invest in your dog's toys wisely – it will define how your pet will look years down the line!

## d. Socialization Arena

The Coton de Tulear can be regarded as a social dog. It usually greets strangers in a warm manner – which poses a question to its guarding capabilities. Nevertheless, you wouldn't need to invest heavily to get your pet accustomed to the city life.

For this small dog, walks in parks and gathering at your home will be sufficient to make it sociable and amiable. If you have any doubts about your pet's behavior, put it on a leash and keep it at a safe distance from other people. Keep it vaccinated regularly to minimize damages in case of an accident. The rest should be fine.

## 4) *Traveling Concerns*

Travel crates are easily the best option available to transport your pet. Make sure it has ample space inside to move a little. Coton de Tulear dogs, seeing their size, will readily adjust with the travel crates. Alternatively, the next best option for you is to employ your personal car!

Public transport, though not really prohibited, will not be a very good idea considering its hyperactive nature. If the place is not too far away, walk your canine companion to its destination – it will be able to get its daily dose of exercise. If this isn't possible, avoid putting other people's lives in danger and use your car instead!

Your car might need a few adjustments to accommodate your pet. Nevertheless, it is an investment worth making – especially if you are a frequent traveler!

Remember to add in identification documents to your dog's collar before leaving home and put it on a leash wherever possible. Keep the windows rolled up so your Coton de Tulear does not feel the impulse to escape.

Also, try to keep it on the back seat to prevent it from interfering with your driving. The ideal scenario is to have someone holding the dog and keeping it distracted.

Coton de Tulear dogs get excited by movement. So naturally having blinds or some toys to keep its eyes away from the windows will be a good idea!

Also, know how your pet signals the call of nature. You definitely do not want reminders of the trip in your car.

Take frequent breaks and walk the Coton de Tulear dog to exhaust its energy reserves. A tired Coton de Tulear is easier to control as compared with one that is full of energy. Improvise along the way as and when required.

There are no hard and fast principles – go with your gut instincts and you should be fine!

After the first few visits, you will automatically find out what more needs to be done to facilitate travels. It isn't a one-time affair. So we suggest you adapt to the rising needs with time!

## 5) *Daily Grooming Guidelines*

The Coton de Tulear is a hairy breed. It has long hairs that are prone to get tangled if not brushed regularly. It is therefore recommended to brush your Coton de Tulear dog's coat multiple times during the day.

The best way is to keep a hair brush in every room where you spend time with your pet. Once it gets busy playing with you or exhibiting its affection for you, just grab the brush and comb its hair. If you have to get up to fetch a brush, it will definitely become a major mood spoiler.

Brush its coat at least twice daily to keep the hairs free from tangles. As far as its bath is concerned, build a monthly schedule that keeps your pet clean and its coat healthy. If your puppy is not much of an inquisitive type, you might delay its shower. See how your pet responds to the grooming needs in order to build a schedule that fits its needs.

Besides this, your Coton de Tulear needs to brush its teeth regularly in order to maintain its dental health. The same goes for ear care though the need to clean its ears becomes more pronounced once it has taken its periodic bath. Invest wisely in eye care as well. Keep in mind that the grooming efforts you make towards your pet define its health and wellness in the present as well as in the future.

# Chapter 12: Training Your Coton de Tulear

The Coton de Tulear is undoubtedly an attractive dog to look at. With its long hair and bubbly nature, it can win anyone's heart! On top of this, the tricks it does to please its onlookers will definitely make it a thousand times more adorable for you!

The Coton de Tulear is generally well behaved and amiable. But to ensure it follows your orders properly and behaves well in front of other people, you need to put it through a robust training regime. Here are a few things you need to keep in mind while planning for its training regime.

## 1) *Your Pet Needs Training*

Most humans believe that they need to take their young dog to puppy classes, and generally speaking, this is a good idea for any young Coton de Tulear (after they have had all their vaccinations), because it will help to get them socialized.

Beyond puppy classes for socializations reasons, hiring a professional dog whisperer for personalized private sessions to train the humans may be far more valuable than training situations where there are multiple dogs and humans together in one class as this can be very distracting for everyone concerned.

## 2) *Puppy Training Basics*

Here are two important and basic aspects of puppy training.

### Three Most Important Words

**"Come"**, **"Sit"** and **"Stay"** will be the three most important words you will ever teach your Coton de Tulear puppy.

110

These three basic commands will ensure that your Coton de Tulear remains safe in almost every circumstance.

For instance, when your puppy correctly learns the "Come" command, you can always quickly bring them back to your side if you should see danger be approaching.

When you teach your Coton de Tulear puppy the "Sit" and "Stay" commands you will be further establishing your leadership role. A puppy that understands that their human guardian is their leader will be a safe and happy follower.

**Choosing a Discipline Sound**

Choosing a *"discipline sound"* that will be the same for every human family member will make it much easier for your puppy to learn what they can or cannot do and will be very useful when warning your Coton de Tulear puppy before they engage in unwanted behavior.

The best types of sounds are short and sharp so that you and your family members can quickly say them and so that the sound will immediately get the attention of your Coton de Tulear puppy because you want to be able to easily interrupt them when they are about to make a mistake.

It doesn't really matter what the sound is, so long as everyone in the family is consistent.

A sound that is very effective for most puppies and dogs is a simple *"UH"* sound said sharply and with emphasis.

Most puppies and dogs respond immediately to this sound and if caught in the middle of doing something they are not supposed to be doing will quickly stop and give you their attention or back away from what they were doing.

## 3) *Acclimatization to the Leash*

**Equipment**: 4 or 6-foot leash, training collar.

The most important ongoing bonding exercise you will experience with your new Coton de Tulear puppy is when you go out for your daily walks together.

Far, far too many people ignore this critical, multi-tasking time that is not only important for your puppy's exercise, it fulfills a multitude of their needs, including:

- Exercising their body
- Fulfilling their natural roaming urges
- Teaching them discipline which engages their mind
- Learning to follow, trust and respect you

As soon as you bring your new puppy home you will want to teach them how to walk at your side while on leash without pulling.

Every time your puppy needs to go out to relieve his or herself, slip on their collar and snap on that leash.

At first your Coton de Tulear puppy may struggle or fight against having a collar around their neck, because the sensation will be new to them. However, at the same time they will want to go with you, so exercise patience and encourage them to walk with you.

Be careful never to drag them, and if they pull backward and refuse to walk forward with you, simply stop for a moment, while keeping slight forward tension on the leash, until your Coton de Tulear puppy gives up and moves forward. Immediately reward them with your happy praise, and if they have a favorite treat, this can be an added incentive when teaching them to walk on their leash.

Always walk your puppy on your left side with the leash slack so that they learn that walking with you is a relaxing experience. Keep the leash short enough so that they do not have enough slack to get in front of you.

If they begin to create tension in the leash by pulling forward or to the side, simply stop moving, get them back beside you, and start over.

Be patient and consistent with your puppy and very soon they will understand exactly where their walking position is and will walk easily beside you without any pulling or leash tension.

Remember that walking with a new puppy is an exciting experience for them as they will want to sniff everything and explore their new world, so give them lots of understanding and don't expect them to be perfect all the time.

When your Coton de Tulear puppy is very young, and wanting to put everything in their mouths, walk them in a harness AND collar and leash, so that you can have a second leash attached to the harness.

All puppies want to put everything in their mouths, therefore, when they are wearing a collar and leash, AND a harness and leash, you will be able to easily lift them over cigarette butts or other garbage you may encounter while out walking.

Once they grow out of the habit of tasting all manner of garbage, you can dispense with the harness and second leash.

## 4) *Walking*

While walking your Coton de Tulear, never let the dog take lead. If it tries to do so, pull strongly at the leash to warn the pet when it is going out of limits. If it still doesn't obey your wishes, stop for a minute and let it follow suit. It will eventually give in to your wishes.

In the same way, if the Coton de Tulear refuses to move, give it time to rethink its decision. It will eventually pick up and start walking by your side if you persist.

Always keep the Coton de Tulear in a following position. You can allow it to talk by your side but make sure it is not mistaking the signal to mean it is ready to lead. If and when it tries to wander off, all you need to do is manipulate its actions by pulling at the leash.

While walking, it is important for you to keep a steady hold on the leash. At the same time, don't pull too hard or drag the puppy with the leash. You might end up strangling the puppy or causing lasting damage to its tender muscles in the neck region. Don't slack but don't pull too hard either.

Take it for a long walk every day. Choose a specific time of the day when the sun is warm and the environment is breathable. It will be an amazing sight to see your Coton de Tulear trot along your side in utter happiness!

## 5) *Penalizing Unwanted Behaviors*

Often humans make the mistake of accidentally rewarding unwanted behaviors.

It is very important to recognize that any attention paid to an overly excited, out of control, adolescent puppy, even negative attention, is likely going to be rewarding for your puppy.

Therefore, when you engage with an out of control Coton de Tulear puppy, you end up actually rewarding them, which will encourage them to continue more of this unwanted behavior.

Be aware that chasing after a puppy when they have taken something they are not supposed to have, picking them up when they are barking or showing aggression, pushing them off when they jump on you or other people, or yelling when they refuse to come when called, are all forms of attention that can actually be rewarding for most puppies.

As your Coton de Tulear dog's guardian, it will be your responsibility to provide calm and consistent structure for your puppy, which will include finding acceptable and safe ways to allow your puppy to vent their energy without being destructive or harmful to property, other dogs, humans, or the actual puppy.

Activities that create or encourage an overly excited Coton de Tulear puppy, such as rough games of tug-o-war, or wild games of chase through the living room, should be immediately curtailed, so that your adolescent puppy learns how to control their energy and play quietly and appropriately without jumping on everyone or engaging in barking or mouthy behavior.

Further, if an adolescent Coton de Tulear puppy displays excited energy simply from being petted by you, your family members or any visitors, you will need to teach yourself, your family and your friends to ignore your puppy until they calm down. Otherwise, you will be teaching your Coton de Tulear puppy that the touch of humans means excitement.

For instance, when you continue to engage with an overly excited puppy, you are rewarding them for out of control behavior and literally teaching them that when they see humans, you want them to display excited energy.

Worse, once your puppy has learned that humans are a source of excitement, you will then have to work very long and hard to reverse this behavior.

Children are often a source of excitement that can cause an adolescent puppy to be extremely wound up.

Do not allow your children to engage with an adolescent Coton de Tulear puppy unless you are there to supervise and teach the children appropriate and calm ways to interact with the puppy.

In order to keep everyone safe, it is very important that your Coton de Tulear puppy learn at an early age that neither children nor adults are sources of excitement.

You can help develop the mind of an adolescent Coton de Tulear and the minds of growing children at the same time by teaching children that your puppy needs structured walks and by showing them how to play fetch, search, hide and seek, or how to teach the Coton de Tulear puppy simple tricks and obedience skills that will be fun and positive interaction for everyone.

## *6) Maintaining Your Patience*

What would you do if your Coton de Tulear dog fails to perform the way you want it to?

Whatever you do, don't shout, holler or physically hurt it. Your Coton de Tulear dog is not a puppet that will follow your orders perfectly every time.

Making mistakes every now and then is perfectly normal for this animal. It will take time and patience to train your Coton de Tulear dog and have it follow your wishes. It does not happen overnight.

So if you are under the impression that training sessions begin yielding results right away, clear the misconception before penalizing your pet.

In any case, if you are penalizing your pet too often on things of no or negligible value, you will end up scarring its personality. The Coton de Tulear dog will become disturbed and develop more behavioral issues. Before getting your pet home, learn to be patient with those that are not subservient to you. Once you've learnt this valuable trait, only then proceed with your Coton de Tulear purchase. Your pet is not something you can abuse simply because you had a bad time at the office; it is a living being just like you. Care and respect it - that is all that it needs!

## 7) Consistency and Perseverance

When you enroll your Coton de Tulear in any of the training lessons, make sure you take it in for the session for the entire duration of the course. Just because your pet apparently seems to be behaving well shouldn't encourage you not to take your pet for further sessions.

For the training sessions to be truly effective and long-lasting, it is important for you to remain consistent with the lessons. For all you know, by missing out on any session, you might be reinforcing negative traits in the Coton de Tulear dog.

Take your pet in for the training lessons regularly. It is best if the lessons are done with during its early years. This helps integrate the lessons and values into the pet's behavior which in turn yields lasting results.

## 8) Using Hand Signals and Speech

Speech training has already been covered in the puppy training basics. Make sure you are putting your pet through the verbal training first. This ensures your pet will be able to follow the hand signals properly when you proceed forward.

Hand signal training is by far the most useful and efficient training method for every dog, including the Coton de Tulear.

This is because all too often we inundate our canine companions with a great deal of chatter and noise that they really do not understand because English is not their first language.

Contrary to what some humans might think, the first language of a Coton de Tulear, or any dog, is a combination of sensing energy and watching body language, which requires no spoken word or sound.

Therefore, when we humans take the time to teach our dog hand signals for all their basic commands, we are communicating with them at a level they instinctively understand, plus we are helping them to become a focused follower, as they must watch us to understand what is required of them.

**Come**: you can kneel down for this command or stay standing. Open your arms wide like you are hugging a very large tree. This hand signal can be seen from a long distance.

When first teaching hand signals to your Coton de Tulear, always show the hand signal for the command at the same time you say the word.

If they are totally ignoring the command, it will be time to incorporate a lunge line, which is a very long leash to help you teach the "Come" command.

Simply attach a 20-foot line to their collar and let them sniff about in a large yard or at your neighborhood park.

At your leisure, firmly ask them to "Come" and show the hand signal. If they do not immediately come to you, give a firm tug with the lunge line, so that they understand what you are asking of them.

If they still do not "Come" toward you, simply reel them in until they are in front of you. Then let them wander about again, until you are ready to ask them to "Come".

Repeat this process until your Coton de Tulear responds correctly at least 80% of the time. You can also reinforce the command by giving a treat when they come back to you when asked. Always ask them to "Sit" when they return to you.

**Sit**: right arm (palm open facing upward) parallel to the floor, and then raise your arm, while bent at the elbow toward your shoulder.

Sit is a very simple, yet extremely valuable command for all puppies and dogs.

If your dog is not sitting on command, try holding a treat above and slightly behind their head, so that when they look up for it they may automatically sit to see it.

Slowly remove the treats as reward and replace the treat with a "life reward", such as a chest rub or a scratch behind the ears and your happy smile.

If your Coton de Tulear is not particularly treat motivated, lift up and slightly back on the leash when asking them to sit (stand in front of them), and if they still are having difficulties, reach down with your free hand, place it across your dog's back at the place where the back legs join the hip and gently squeeze.

Remember -- Do NOT simply push down on your dog's back to force their hind legs to collapse under them as this pressure could harm their spine or leg joints.

**Stay**: right arm fully extended toward your dog's head, palm open, hand bent up at the wrist.

Once your Coton de Tulear is in the "Sit" position, ask them to "Stay" with both the verbal cue and the hand signal.

**TIP**: if you are right-handed, use your right arm and hand for the signal, and if you are left-handed, use your left arm and hand for the signal. Using your dominant hand will be much more effective because your strongest energy emanates from the palm of your dominant hand.

While your dog is sitting and staying, slowly back away from them. If they move from their position, calmly put them back into Sit and ask them to "Stay" again, using both the verbal cue and the hand signal.

Continue to practice this until your dog understands that you want them to stay sitting and not move toward you.

With all commands, when your Coton de Tulear is just learning, be patient and always reward them with a treat and your happy praise for a job well done.

## 9) Adult Training

The adolescent period in a young Coton de Tulear dog's life, between the ages of 6 and 12 months, is the transitional stage of both physical and psychological development when they are physically almost full grown in size, yet their minds are still developing and they are testing their boundaries and the limits that their human counterparts will endure.

This can be a dangerous time in a puppy's life because this is when they start to make decisions on their own which, if they do not receive the leadership they need from their human guardians, can lead to developing unwanted behaviors.

When living within a human environment, your puppy must always adhere to human rules and it will be up to their human guardians to continue their vigilant, watchful guidance in order to make sure that they do.

Many humans are lulled into a false sense of security when their new Coton de Tulear puppy reaches the age of approximately six months, because the puppy has been well socialized, they have been to puppy classes and long since been house trained.

The real truth is that the serious work is only now beginning and the humans and their new Coton de Tulear puppy could be in for a time of testing that could seriously challenge the relationship and leave the humans wondering if they made the right decision to share their home with a dog.

If the human side of the relationship is not prepared for this transitional time in their young dog's life, their patience may be seriously tried, and the relationship of trust and respect that has been previously built can be damaged, and could take considerable time to repair.

While not all adolescent puppies will experience a noticeable adolescent period of craziness, because every puppy is different, most young dogs do commonly exhibit at least some of the usual adolescent behaviors, including reverting to previous puppy behaviors.

Some of these adolescent behaviors might include destructive chewing of objects they have previously shown no interest in, selective hearing or ignoring previously learned commands, displaying aggressive behavior, jumping on everyone, barking at everything that moves, or reverting to relieving themselves in the house, even though they were house trained months ago.

Keeping your cool and recognizing these adolescent signs are the first steps toward helping to make this transition period easier on your Coton de Tulear puppy and all family members.

The first step to take that can help keep raging hormones at bay, is to spay or neuter your Coton de Tulear puppy just prior to the onset of adolescence, at around four or five months of age.

While spaying or neutering a Coton de Tulear puppy will not entirely eliminate the adolescent phase, it will certainly help and at the same time will spare your puppy the added strain of both the physical and emotional changes that occur during sexual maturity.

As well, some female puppies will become extremely aggressive toward other dogs during a heat, and non-neutered males may become territorially aggressive and pick fights with other males.

Once your Coton de Tulear puppy has been spayed or neutered, you will want to become more active with your young dog, both mentally and physically by providing them with continued and more complex disciplined exercises.

This can be accomplished by enrolling your adolescent Coton de Tulear in a dog whispering session or more advanced training class, which will help them to continue their socialization skills while also developing their brain.

Even though it may be more difficult to train during this period, having the assistance of a professional and continuing the experience of ongoing socialization amongst other dogs of a similar size can be invaluable, as this is the time when many young dogs begin to show signs of antisocial behavior with other dogs as well as unknown humans.

When your Coton de Tulear is provided with sufficient daily exercise and continued socialization with unfamiliar dogs, people and places that provides interest and expands their mind, they will be able to transition through the adolescent stage of their life much more seamlessly.

## *10) Handling Behavioral Issues*

It can be difficult, if not impossible to generalize or speculate with respect to alleviating possible behavioral issues or problems because, in most cases, a dog suffering from behavioral issues requires the assistance of a dog whisperer or dog psychologist.

When reading anything about how to prevent or cure behavioral issues, please be aware that behavioral problems most often cannot be properly assessed or cured by reading a book.

The reason for this is because there are just too many variables and unique situations, individual dogs, individual humans, unique circumstances, and endless reasons why they may have developed any particular behavioral issue.

Therefore, without knowing the dog's particulars and all the history of what has transpired between the Coton de Tulear and their guardian that came before, attempting to write about how to cure a particular issue will be no more than a best guess.

This is why someone whose dog is suffering from a specific behavioral issue that is in turn, at the least embarrassing, or at the worst, driving the humans and the entire neighborhood crazy, must be properly addressed by engaging the services of a professional dog whisperer (psychologist or behaviorist) who can ask many questions, properly assess the situation and then design a unique plan for alleviating the problem.

## *11) Human Training*

House training, house breaking, or *"potty"* training, is a critical first step in the education of any new puppy, and the first part of a successful process is training the human guardian.

When you bring home your new Coton de Tulear puppy, they will be relying upon your guidance to teach them what they need to learn.

When you provide your puppy with your consistent patience and understanding, they are capable of learning rules at a very early age, and house training is no different, especially since it's all about establishing a regular routine.

Potty training a new puppy takes time and patience — how much time depends entirely upon you.

Check in with yourself and make sure your energy remains consistently calm and patient and that you exercise plenty of compassion and understanding while you help your new puppy learn their new bathroom rules.

Coton de Tulear puppies and dogs flourish with routines and happily, so do humans, therefore, the first step is to establish a daily routine that will work well for both canine and human alike.

For instance, depending upon the age of your Coton de Tulear puppy, make a plan to take them out for a bathroom break every two hours and stick to it because while you are in the beginning stages of potty training, the more vigilant and consistent you can be, the quicker and more successful your results will be.

Generally speaking, while your puppy is still growing, a young puppy can hold it approximately one hour for every month of their age.

This means that if your 2-month-old puppy has been happily snoozing for a couple of hours, as soon as they wake up, they will need to go outside.

Some of the first indications or signs that your puppy needs to be taken outside to relieve themselves will be when you see them:

- sniffing around
- circling
- looking for the door
- whining, crying or barking
- acting agitated

It will be important to always take your Coton de Tulear puppy out first thing every morning, and immediately after they wake up from a nap as well as soon after they have finished eating a meal or having a big drink of water.

Also, your happy praise goes a long way toward encouraging and reinforcing future success when your Coton de Tulear puppy makes the right decisions, so let them know you are happy when they do their business in the right place.

Initially, treats can be a good way to reinforce how pleased you are that your puppy is learning to go potty in the right place. Slowly treats can be removed and replaced with your happy praise.

Next, now that you have a new puppy in your life, you will want to be flexible with respect to adapting your schedule to meet the requirements that will help to quickly teach your Coton de Tulear puppy their new bathroom routine.

This means not leaving your puppy alone for endless hours at a time because firstly, they are sensitive pack animals that need companionship and your direction at all times, plus long periods alone will result in the disruption of the potty training schedule you have worked hard to establish.

If you have no choice but to leave your puppy alone for many hours, make sure that you place them in a paper lined room or pen where they can relieve themselves without destroying your favorite carpet or new hardwood flooring.

Remember, your Coton de Tulear is a growing puppy with a bladder and bowels that they do not yet have complete control over and you will have a much happier time and better success if you simply train yourself to pay attention to when your young companion is showing signs of needing to relieve themselves.

## *12) Bell Training*

A very easy way to introduce your new Coton de Tulear puppy to house training is to begin by teaching them how to ring a doorbell whenever they need to go outside.

Ringing a doorbell is not only a convenient alert system for both you and your Coton de Tulear puppy or dog, your visitors will be most impressed by how smart your Coton de Tulear is.

A further benefit of training your puppy to ring a bell is that you will not have to listen to your puppy or dog whining, barking or howling to be let out, and your door will not become scratched from their nails.

Unless you prefer to purchase an already manufactured doggy doorbell or system, take a trip to your local novelty store and purchase a small bell that has a nice, loud ring.

Attach the bell to a piece of ribbon or string and hang it from a door handle or tape it to a door sill near the door where you will be taking your puppy out when they need to relieve themselves. The string will need to be long enough so that your Coton de Tulear puppy can easily reach the bell with their nose or a paw.

Next, each time you take your puppy out to go potty, say the word *"Out"*, and use their paw or their nose to ring the bell. Praise them for this *"trick"* and immediately take them outside.

The only down side to teaching your Coton de Tulear puppy or dog to ring a bell when they want to go outside, is that even if they don't actually have to go out to relieve themselves, but just want to go outside because they are bored, you will still have to take them out every time they ring the bell.

There are many types and styles of *"gotta' go"* commercially manufactured bells you could choose, ranging from the elegant **"Poochie Bells™"** that hang from a doorknob, the simple **"Tell Bell™"** that sits on the floor, or various high tech door chime systems that function much like a doggy intercom system where they push a pad with their paw and it rings a bell.

Whatever doorbell system you choose for your Coton de Tulear puppy, once they are trained, this type of an alert system is an easy way to eliminate accidents in the home.

## 13)   *Kennel Training*

Kennel training is always a good idea for any puppy early in their education because it can be utilized for many different situations, including keeping them safe while traveling inside a vehicle and being a very helpful tool for house training.

When purchasing a kennel for your Coton de Tulear puppy, always buy a kennel that will be the correct size for your puppy once they become an adult.

The kennel will be the correct size if an adult Coton de Tulear can stand up and easily turn around inside their kennel.

When you train your Coton de Tulear puppy to accept sleeping in their own kennel at nighttime, this will also help to accelerate their potty training, because no puppy or dog wants to relieve themselves where they sleep, which means that they will hold their bladder and bowels as long as they possibly can.

Always be kind and compassionate and remember that a puppy will be able to hold it approximately one hour for every month of their age.

Generally, a Coton de Tulear puppy that is three months old will be able to hold it for approximately three hours, unless they just ate a meal or had a big drink of water.

Be watchful and consistent so that you learn your Coton de Tulear puppy's body language, which will alert you to when it's time for them to go outside.

Presenting them with familiar scents, by taking them to the same spot in the yard or the same street corner, will help to remind and encourage them that they are outside to relieve themselves.

Use a voice cue to remind your puppy why they are outside, such as *"go pee"* and always remember to praise them every time they relieve themselves in the right place so that they quickly understand what you expect of them and will learn to *"go"* on cue.

## *14)  Exercise Pen Training*

The exercise pen is a transition from kennel only training and will be helpful for those times when you may have to leave your Coton de Tulear puppy for more hours than they can reasonably be expected to hold it.

During those times when you must be away from the home for several hours, it's time to introduce your Coton de Tulear puppy to an exercise pen.

Exercise pens are usually constructed of wire sections that you can put together in whatever shape you desire, and the pen needs to be large enough to hold your puppy's kennel inside one half of the pen, while the other half will be lined with newspapers or pee pads.

Place your Coton de Tulear puppy's food and water dishes next to the kennel and leave the kennel door open, so they can wander in and out whenever they wish, to eat or drink or go to the papers or pads if they need to relieve themselves.

Your puppy will be contained in a small area of your home while you are away and because they are already used to sleeping inside their kennel, they will not want to relieve themselves inside the area where they sleep. Therefore, your Coton de Tulear puppy will naturally go to the other half of the pen to relieve themselves on the newspapers or pee pads.

This method will help train your puppy to be quickly "paper" trained when you must leave them alone for a few hours.

## 15)  *Puppy Apartment™ Training*

A similar and more costly alternative, the *Puppy Apartment™* is a step up from the exercise pen training system that makes the process of crate or pen training even easier on both humans and puppies.

The Puppy Apartment™ works well in a variety of situations, whether you're at home and unable to pay close attention to your Coton de Tulear puppy's needs, whether you must be away from the home for a few hours or during the evening when everyone is asleep and you don't particularly want to get up at 3:00 a.m. to take your Coton de Tulear puppy out to go pee.

The Puppy Apartment™ is an innovation that is convenient for both puppy and human alike.

What makes this system so effective is the patent pending dividing wall with a door leading to the other side, all inside the pen.

One side of the Puppy Apartment™ is where the puppy's bed is located and the other side (through the doorway) is the bathroom area that is lined with pee pads.

With the bathroom right next door, your Coton de Tulear puppy or dog can take a bathroom break whenever they wish, without the need to alert family members to let them out.

This one bedroom, one bathroom system, which is a combination of the kennel/training pen, is a great alternative for helping to eliminate the stress of worrying about always keeping a watchful eye on your puppy or getting up during the night to take them outside every few hours to help them avoid making mistakes.

According to "Modern Puppies":

*"The Puppy Apartment™ takes the MESSY out of paper training, the ODORS AND HASSLES out of artificial grass training, MISSING THE MARK out of potty pad training and HAVING TO HOLD IT out of crate training. House training a puppy has never been faster or easier!*

*The Puppy Apartment™ has taken all the benefits of the most popular potty training methods and combined them into one magical device and potty training system. This device and system has revolutionized how modern puppies are potty trained!"*

Manufactured in the United States, this product ships directly from the California suppliers (Modern Puppies).

Pricing of the Puppy Apartment™ begins at $138. USD (£83.37) and is only available online at Modern Puppies.

## *16)   Free Training*

If you would rather not confine your young Coton de Tulear puppy to one or two rooms in your home, and will be allowing them to freely range about your home anywhere they wish during the day, this is considered free training.

When free house training your Coton de Tulear puppy, you will need to closely watch your puppy's activities all day long so that you can be aware of the *"signs"* that will indicate when they need to go outside to relieve themselves.

For instance, circling and sniffing is a sure sign that they are looking for a place to do their business.

Never get upset or scold a puppy for having an accident inside the home, because this will result in teaching your puppy to be afraid of you and to only relieve themselves in secret places or when you're not watching.

If you catch your Coton de Tulear puppy making a mistake, all that is necessary is for you to calmly say *"No"*, and quickly scoop them up and take them outside or to their indoor bathroom area.

From your sensitive puppy's point of view, yelling or screaming when they make a potty mistake, will be understood by your puppy or dog as unstable energy being displayed by the person who is supposed to be their leader. This type of unstable behavior will only teach your puppy to fear and disrespect you.

When you are vigilant, the Coton de Tulear is not a difficult puppy to housebreak and they will generally do very well when you start them off with *"puppy pee pads"* that you will move closer and closer to the same door that you always use when taking them outside. This way they will quickly learn to associate going to this door when they need to relieve themselves.

When you pay close attention to your Coton de Tulear puppy's sleeping, eating, drinking and playing habits, you will quickly learn their body language so that you are able to predict when they might need to relieve themselves.

Your Coton de Tulear puppy will always need to relieve themselves first thing in the morning, as soon as they wake up from a nap, approximately 20 minutes after they finish eating a meal, after they have finished a play session, and of course, before they go to bed at night.

It's important to have compassion during this house training time in your young Coton de Tulear's life so that their education will be as stress-free as possible.

It's also important to be vigilant because how well you pay attention will minimize the opportunities your puppy may have for making a bathroom mistake in the first place, and the fewer mistakes they make, the sooner your Coton de Tulear puppy will be house trained.

## *17) Electronic Devices Training*

Generally speaking, positive training methods are far more effective than using devices that involve negative stimulation.

Further, unless you are training a Coton de Tulear to hunt badgers or rabbits, using electronic devices is usually an excuse for a lazy human who will not take the time to properly train their dog by teaching them rules and boundaries which leads to respect and an attentive follower.

When you do not provide your Coton de Tulear (or any dog) with a consistent leadership role that teaches your dog to trust, respect and listen to you in all circumstances, you will inevitably experience behavioral issues.

Electronic training devices such as e-collars, spray collars or electronic fencing all rely upon negative, painful or stressful reinforcement, which can easily cause a sensitive breed, like the Coton de Tulear, to become nervous or live a life of fear.

For instance, a dog simply cannot understand the principles of "invisible" boundaries, and therefore, should never be subjected to the confusion of the punishment that occurs when walking across an invisible line within their own home territory.

Dogs naturally understand the positive training methods of receiving a reward, which is not only much more efficient and effective when teaching boundaries, rewards are far kinder, and create a much stronger bond with your dog.

**The Truth About Shock Collars**

First of all, it would have to be an extremely rare situation in which it would be necessary or recommended that you use a shock collar on a small Coton de Tulear as these devices are usually only employed in extreme situations, and generally for much larger breeds who could seriously harm someone.

The use of remote, electronic, shock or *"e-collars"* is at best a controversial subject that can quickly escalate into heated arguments.

In certain, rare circumstances, and when used correctly, the e-collar can be a helpful training tool that could actually save a dog's life if they are acting out in dangerous ways.

An e-collar would generally be utilized in a circumstance where a larger breed of dog has access to free range over a large property, resulting in difficulties getting their attention from a distance if they become distracted by other animals or smells.

Many dogs that not been properly trained from a young age also learn that when they are off leash and out of your immediate reach that they can choose to ignore your commands, bark their heads off, terrorize the neighbors or chase wildlife.

All of these situations are generally not activities that a Coton de Tulear would have the slightest interest in because they love being at home with their humans.

Generally e-collars can be effective training tools for working breed herding or hunting or tracking dogs.

In these types of circumstances a remote training collar can be an effective training device for reinforcing verbal commands from a great distance, such as "Come", "Sit" or "Stay".

Finally, electronic collars can be used as a last resort to help teach a dog not to engage in a dangerous behavior that could result in them being seriously harmed or even killed.

**Electronic Fencing**

Honestly, there are far more reasons NOT to install an electronic fence as a means of keeping your dog inside your yard, than there are good reasons for considering one.

For instance, a dog whose yard is surrounded by an electronic fence can quite easily develop fear, aggression, or both, directed toward what they may believe is the cause of the shock they are receiving.

As a result, installing an electronic fence may cause your Coton de Tulear to become aggressive toward cats, other dogs, other humans, other wildlife, children riding by on bikes or skateboards, the mail carrier, or the dog next door.

As well, a dog that receives a fright, or one who is in a state of excitement forgets about the shock they are going to receive, may run through an electronic fence and then be too frightened or stressed to come back home because it means that they must pass through the painful barrier again.

Further, it is actually possible that electronic fencing may encourage a dog to escape the yard simply because they associate their yard with pain. This feeling can be reinforced if a dog escapes the electronic yard and then is again punished by the shock when they attempt to come home.

Another factor to keep in mind with respect to electronic fencing is that other dogs or teasing children can freely enter the yard and torment or attack your dog, and a thief bent on stealing your Coton de Tulear will be able to do so with ease.

The absolute best way to keep your dog safe in their own yard, while helping to establish your role as guardian and leader, is to be out there with them while they are on leash, and to only permit them freedom in your yard under your close supervision.

## 18) *Simple Tips and Tricks for Training*

When teaching your Coton de Tulear tricks, in order to give them extra incentive, find a treat that they really like, and give the treat as rewards and to help solidify a good performance.

Most dogs will be extra attentive during training sessions when they know that they will be rewarded with their favorite treats.

If your Coton de Tulear is less than six months old when you begin teaching them tricks, keep your training sessions short (no more than 5 or 10 minutes) and fun, and as they become adults, you can extend your sessions as they will be able to maintain their focus for longer periods of time.

**Shake a Paw**

Who doesn't love a dog that knows how to shake a paw? This is one of the easiest tricks to teach your Coton de Tulear.

**TIP**: most dogs are naturally either right or left pawed. If you know which paw your dog favours, ask them to shake this paw.

Find a quiet place to practice, without noisy distractions or other pets, and stand or sit in front of your dog. Place them in the sitting position and have a treat in your left hand.

Say the command *"Shake"* while putting your right hand behind their left or right paw and pulling the paw gently toward yourself until you are holding their paw in your hand. Immediately praise them and give them the treat.

Most dogs will learn the "Shake" trick very quickly, and very soon, once you put out your hand, your Coton de Tulear will immediately lift their paw and put it into your hand, without your assistance or any verbal cue.

Practice every day until they are 100% reliable with this trick, and then it will be time to add another trick to their repertoire.

**Roll Over**

You will find that just like your Coton de Tulear is naturally either right or left pawed, that they will also naturally want to roll either to the right or the left side. Take advantage of this by asking your dog to roll to the side they naturally prefer.

Sit with your dog on the floor and put them in a lie down position. Hold a treat in your hand and place it close to their nose without allowing them to grab it, and while they are in the lying position, move the treat to the right or left side of their head so that they have to roll over to get to it.

You will very quickly see which side they want to naturally roll to, and once you see this, move the treat to this side. Once they roll over to this side, immediately give them the treat and praise them.

You can say the verbal cue *"Over"* while you demonstrate the hand signal motion (moving your right hand in a circular motion) or moving the treat from one side of their head to the other with a half circle motion.

**Roll Over**: moving your right or left arm/hand in a small circular motion, in the direction you wish your dog to roll toward.

Once your Coton de Tulear can roll over every time you ask, it will be time to teach them another trick.

**Sit Pretty**

While this trick is a little more complicated, and most dogs pick up on it very quickly, remember that every dog is different so always exercise patience.

Find a quiet space with few distractions and sit or stand in front of your dog and ask them to "Sit".

Have a treat nearby (on a countertop or table) and when they sit, use both of your hands to lift up their front paws into the sitting pretty position, while saying the command *"Sit Pretty"*. Help them balance in this position while you praise them and give them the treat.

Once your Coton de Tulear can do the balancing part of the trick quite easily without your help, sit or stand in front of your dog while asking them to *"Sit Pretty"* and hold the treat above their head, at the level their nose would be when they sit pretty.

**TIP**: when first beginning this trick, place your Coton de Tulear beside a wall so they can use the wall to help them balance.

If they attempt to stand on their back legs to get the treat, you may be holding the treat too high, which will encourage them to stand on their back legs to reach it. Go back to the first step and put them back into the *"Sit"* position and again lift their paws while their backside remains on the floor.

**Sit Pretty**: hold your straight arm, fully extended, over your dog's head with a closed fist.

Make this a fun and entertaining time for your Coton de Tulear and practice a few times every day until they can *"Sit Pretty"* on hand signal command every time you ask.

A young Coton de Tulear puppy should be able to easily learn these basic tricks before they are six months old and when you are patient and make your training sessions short and fun for your dog, they will be eager to learn more.

## 19)    *Handling Mistake While Training*

Remember that a dog's sense of smell is at least 2,000 times more sensitive that our human sense of smell.

As a result of your Coton de Tulear puppy's superior sense of smell, it will be very important to effectively remove all odors from house training accidents, because otherwise, your Coton de Tulear puppy will be attracted by the smell to the place where they may have had a previous accident, and will want to do their business there again and again.

While there are many products that are supposed to remove odors and stains, many of these are not very effective. You want a professional grade cleaner that will not just mask one odor with another scent; you want a product that will completely neutralize odors.

**TIP**: go to RemoveUrineOdors.com and order yourself some *"SUN"* and/or *"Max Enzyme"* because these products contain professional-strength odor neutralizers and urine digesters that bind to and completely absorb odors on any type of surface.

# Chapter 13: Medical Concerns

The medical condition of your dog is another major concern for the health and well being of your pet. Make sure you are reading through this section carefully and are fully aware of your responsibilities as the owner of a Coton de Tulear dog. Any ignorance in this aspect can seriously damage your puppy's health. Here are a couple of things you should keep in mind in this respect.

## 1) Tips for choosing a Veterinarian

A consideration to keep in mind when choosing a veterinarian clinic will be that some clinics specialize in caring for smaller pets, and some specialize in larger animal care, while still others have a wide ranging area of expertise and will care for all animals, including livestock and reptiles.

Choosing a clinic will be a personal decision, however, since the Coton de Tulear is considered a smaller breed of dog, your dog's needs may be better served by choosing a clinic that specializes in the care of smaller pets.

Choosing a good veterinary clinic will be very similar to choosing the right health care clinic or doctor for your own personal health because you want to ensure that your Coton de Tulear puppy receives the quality care they deserve.

Begin your search by asking other dog owners where they take their fur friends and whether they are happy with the service they receive.

If you don't know anyone to ask, visit the local pet store in your area as they should be able to provide you with references and local listings of pet care clinics.

Next, check online, because a good pet clinic will have an active website up and running that will list details of all the services they provide along with an overview of all staff members, their education and qualifications.

Once you've narrowed your search, it's time to personally visit the clinics you may be interested in, as this will be a good opportunity for you to visually inspect the facility, interact with the staff and perhaps meet the veterinarians face to face.

Of course, it's not just you who needs to feel comfortable with the clinic chosen and those working there. Your puppy needs to feel comfortable, too, and this is where visiting a clinic and interacting with the staff and veterinarians will provide you with an idea of their experience and expertise in handling your puppy.

If your puppy is comfortable with them, then you will be much more likely to trust that they will be providing the best care for your puppy that will need to receive all their vaccinations and yearly check-ups, and eventually be spayed or neutered.

It's also a good idea to take your puppy into your chosen clinic several times before they actually need to be there for any treatment, so that they are not fearful of the new smells and unfamiliar surroundings.

## 2) Neutering and Spaying

While it can sometimes be difficult to find the definitive answer when asking when is the best time to neuter or spay your young Coton de Tulear, because there are varying opinions on this topic, one thing that most veterinarians do agree on is that earlier spaying or neutering, between 4 and 6 months of age, is a better choice than waiting.

Spaying or neutering surgeries are carried out under general anesthesia, and as more dogs are being neutered at younger ages, speak with your veterinarian and ask for their recommendations regarding the right age to spay or neuter your Coton de Tulear.

**Effects on Aggression**

Intact (non-neutered) males and females are more likely to display aggression related to sexual behavior than are dogs that have been neutered or spayed.

Fighting, particularly in male dogs that are directed at other males, is less common after neutering, and the intensity of other types of aggression, such as irritable aggression in females will be totally eliminated by spaying.

While neutering or spaying is not a treatment for aggression, it can certainly help to minimize the severity and escalation of aggressiveness and is often the first step toward resolving an aggressive behavior problem.

**What is Neutering?**

Neutering is a surgical procedure, carried out by a licensed veterinarian surgeon to render a male dog unable to reproduce.

In males, the surgery is also referred to as *"castration"* because the procedure entails the removal of the young dog's testicles. When the testicles are removed, what is left behind is an empty scrotal sac (which used to contain the puppy's testicles) and this empty sac will soon shrink in size until it is no longer noticeable.

**Neutering Males**

Neutering male Coton de Tulear puppies before they are six months of age can help to ensure that they will be less likely to suffer from obesity problems when they grow older.

Neutering can also mean that a male Coton de Tulear will be less likely to have the urge to wander.

Further, waiting until a male Coton de Tulear is older than six months before having them neutered could mean that they will experience the effects of raging testosterone that will drive them to escape their yards by any means necessary to search out females to mate with.

Non-neutered males also tend to spray or mark territory much more often, both inside and outside the home, and during this time can start to display aggressive tendencies toward other dogs as well as people.

## What is Spaying?

In female puppies, sterilization, referred to as *"spaying"* is a surgical procedure carried out by a licensed veterinarian, to prevent the female dog from becoming pregnant and to stop regular heat cycles.

The sterilization procedure is much more involved for a female puppy (than for a male), as it requires the removal of both ovaries and the uterus by incision into the puppy's abdominal cavity. The uterus is also removed during this surgery, to prevent the possibility of it becoming infected later on in life.

## Spaying Females

Preferably, female Coton de Tulear puppies should be spayed before their very first estrus or heat cycle. Females in heat often appear more agitated and irritable, while sleeping and eating less and some may become extremely aggressive toward other dogs.

Spaying female puppies before their first heat pattern can eliminate these hormonal stressors and reduce the opportunity of mammary glandular tumors. Early spaying also protects against various other potential concerns, such as uterine infections.

## Effects on General Temperament

Many dog owners often become needlessly worried that a neutered or spayed dog will lose their vigor.

Rest assured that a dog's personality or energy level will not be modified or altered in any way by the neutering process, and in fact, many unfavorable qualities resulting from hormonal impact may resolve after surgery.

Your Coton de Tulear will certainly not come to be less caring or cheerful, and neither will he or she resent you because you are not denying your dog any essential encounters. You will, however, be acting as a conscientious, informed, and caring Coton de Tulear guardian.

Further, there is little evidence to suggest that the nature of a female Coton de Tulear will improve after having a litter of puppies.

What is important is that you do not project your own psychological needs or concerns onto your Coton de Tulear puppy, because there is no gain to be had from permitting sexual activity in either male or female canines.

For instance, it is not *"abnormal"* or *"mean"* to manage a puppy's reproductive activity by having them sterilized. Rather, it is unkind and irresponsible not to neuter or spay a dog and there are many positive benefits of having this procedure carried out.

**Effects on Escape and Roaming**

A neutered or spayed Coton de Tulear is less likely to wander. Castrated male dogs have the tendency to patrol smaller sized outdoor areas and are less likely to participate in territorial conflicts with perceived opponents.

**NOTE**: a Coton de Tulear that has actually already experienced successful escapes from the yard may continue to wander after they are spayed or neutered.

## Effects on Problem Elimination

An unsterilized dog may urinate or defecate inside the home or in other undesirable areas in an attempt to stake territorial claims, relieve anxiety, or advertise their available reproductive status.

While neutering or spaying a Coton de Tulear puppy after they have already begun to inappropriately eliminate or mark territory to announce their sexual availability to other dogs will reduce the more powerful urine odor as well as eliminate the hormonal factors, once this habit has begun, the undesirable behavior may continue to persist after neutering or spaying.

## Possible Weight Gain

While metabolic changes that occur after spaying or neutering can cause some Coton de Tulear puppy's to gain weight, often the real culprit for any weight gain is the human who feels guilty for subjecting their puppy to any kind of pain and therefore, they attempt to make themselves feel better by feeding more treats or meals to their Coton de Tulear companion.

If you are concerned about weight gain after neutering or spaying a Coton de Tulear puppy, simply adjust their food and treat consumption, as needed, and make sure that they receive adequate daily exercise.

It's a very simply process to change your Coton de Tulear dog's food intake according to their physical demands and how they look, and if your Coton de Tulear puppy's daily exercise and level of activity has not changed after they have been spayed or neutered, there will likely be no change in food management necessary.

## 3) Vaccinations

Puppies need to be vaccinated by a veterinarian in order to provide them with protection against four common and serious diseases.

Vaccination against this common set of diseases is referred to as *"DAPP"*, which stands for **D**istemper, **A**denovirus, **P**arainfluenza and **P**arvo Virus.

Approximately one week after your Coton de Tulear puppy has completed all three sets of primary DAPP vaccinations they will be fully protected from those specific diseases. Thereafter, most veterinarians will recommend a once a year vaccination for the next year or two.

It has now become common practice to vaccinate adult dogs every three years, and if your veterinarian is insisting on a yearly vaccination for your Coton de Tulear puppy, you need to ask them why, because to do otherwise is considered by most professionals to be *"over vaccinating"*.

**Distemper**

Canine distemper is a contagious and serious viral illness for which there is currently no known cure.

This deadly virus, which is spread either through the air or by direct or indirect contact with a dog that is already infected or other distemper carrying wildlife, including ferrets, raccoons, foxes, skunks and wolves, is a relative of the measles virus which affects humans.

Canine distemper is sometimes also called *"hard pad disease"* because some strains of the distemper virus actually cause thickening of the pads on a dog's feet, which can also affect the end of a dog's nose.

In dogs or animals with weak immune systems, death may result two to five weeks after the initial distemper infection.

Early symptoms of distemper include fever, loss of appetite, and mild eye inflammation that may only last a day or two. Symptoms become more serious and noticeable as the disease progresses.

A puppy or dog that survives the distemper virus will usually continue to experience symptoms or signs of the disease throughout their remaining lifespan, including *"hard pad disease"* as well as *"enamel hypoplasia"*, which is damage to the enamel of the puppy's teeth that are not yet formed or that have not yet pushed through the gums.

Enamel hypoplasia is caused when the distemper virus kills the cells that manufacture tooth enamel.

**Adenovirus**

It is a virus that causes infectious canine hepatitis, which can range in severity from very mild to very serious, sometimes resulting in death.

Symptoms can include coughing, loss of appetite, increased thirst and urination, tiredness, runny eyes and nose, vomiting, bruising or bleeding under the skin, swelling of the head, neck and body, fluid accumulation in the abdomen area, jaundice (yellow tinge to the skin), a bluish clouding of the cornea of the eye (called "hepatitis blue eye") and seizures.

There is no specific treatment for infectious canine hepatitis. Treatment of the disease is focused on managing symptoms while the virus runs its course. Hospitalization and intravenous fluid therapy may be required in severe cases.

**Canine Parainfluenza Virus**

The canine parainfluenza virus (CPIV) also referred to as *"canine influenza virus"*, *"greyhound disease"* or *"race flu"*, which is easily spread through the air or by coming into contact with respiratory secretions, was originally a virus that only affected horses.

This disease is believed to have adapted to become contagious to dogs, is easily spread from dog to dog, and may cause symptoms that become fatal.

While the more frequent occurrences of this respiratory infection are seen in areas where there are high dog populations, such as race tracks, boarding kennels and pet stores, this virus is highly contagious to any dog or puppy, at any age.

Symptoms can include a dry, hacking cough, difficulty breathing, wheezing, runny nose and eyes, sneezing, fever, loss of appetite, tiredness, depression and possible pneumonia.

In cases where only a cough exists, tests will be required to determine whether the cause of the cough is the parainfluenza virus or the less serious *"kennel cough"*.

While many dogs can naturally recover from this virus, they will remain contagious, and for this reason, in order to prevent the spread to other animals, aggressive treatment of the virus, with antibiotics and antiviral drugs will be the general course of action.

In more severe cases, a cough suppressant may be prescribed, as well as intravenous fluids to help prevent secondary bacterial infection.

**Canine Parvovirus**

Canine parvovirus (CPV) is a highly contagious viral illness affecting puppies and dogs. Parvovirus also affects other canine species including foxes, coyotes and wolves.

There are two forms of this virus (1) the more common intestinal form, and (2) the less common cardiac form, which can cause death in young puppies.

Symptoms of the intestinal form of parvovirus include vomiting, bloody diarrhea, weight loss, and lack of appetite, while the less common cardiac form attacks the heart muscle.

Early vaccination in young puppies has radically reduced the incidence of canine parvovirus infection, which is easily transmitted either by direct contact with an infected dog, or indirectly, by sniffing an infected dog's feces.

The virus can also be brought into a dog's environment on the bottom of human shoes that may have stepped on infected feces, and there is evidence that this hardy virus can live in ground soil for up to a year.

Recovery from parvovirus requires both aggressive and early treatment. With proper treatment, death rates are relatively low (between 5 and 20%), although chances of survival for puppies are much lower than for older dogs, and in all instances, there is no guarantee of survival.

Treatment of parvovirus requires hospitalization where intravenous fluids and nutrients are administered to help combat dehydration. As well, antibiotics will be given to counteract secondary bacterial infections, and as necessary, medications to control nausea and vomiting may also be given.

Without prompt and proper treatment, dogs that have severe parvovirus infections can die within 48 to 72 hours.

## 4) *Diseases and Viruses to Look Out For*

### a) Rabies

Rabies is a viral disease transmitted by coming into contact with the saliva of an infected animal, usually through a bite.

The virus travels to the brain along the nerves and once symptoms develop, death is almost certainly inevitable, usually following a prolonged period of suffering.

If you plan to travel out of State or across country borders, you will need to make sure that your Coton de Tulear has an up to date Rabies Vaccination Certificate (NASPHV form 51) indicating they have been inoculated against rabies.

Vaccinating dogs against rabies is also compulsory in most countries in mainland Europe, as is permanent identification and registration of dogs through the use of a Pet Passport.

Those living in a country that is rabies free (UK, Eire) are not required to vaccinate their dogs against rabies, unless they intend to travel.

## b) Leishmaniasis

Leishmaniasis is caused by a parasite and is transmitted by a bite from a sand fly.

There is no definitive answer for effectively combating Leishmaniasis, especially since one vaccine will not prevent the known multiple species.

In areas where the known cause is a sand fly, deltamethrin collars (containing a neurotoxic insecticide) worn by the dogs has been proven to be 86% effective.

There are two types of Leishmaniasis: (1) a skin reaction causing hair loss, lesions and ulcerative dermatitis, and (2) a more severe, abdominal organ reaction, which is also known as *"black fever"*. When the disease affects organs of the abdominal cavity the symptoms include:

- loss of appetite
- diarrhea

- severe weight loss
- exercise intolerance
- vomiting
- nose bleed
- tarry feces
- fever
- pain in the joints
- excessive thirst and urination
- inflammation of the muscles

Leishmaniasis spreads throughout the body to most organs, with kidney failure being the most common cause of death. Virtually all infected dogs develop this system wide disease and as much as 90% of those infected will also display skin reactions.

Affected dogs in the US are frequently found to have acquired this infection in another country.

Of note, is that this disease is regularly found in the Middle East, the area around the Mediterranean basin, Portugal, Spain, Africa, South and Central America, southern Mexico and the US, with regular cases reported in Oklahoma and Ohio, where it is found in 20 to 40% of the dog population.

There have also been a few reported cases in Switzerland, northern France and the Netherlands.

**NOTE:** Leishmaniasis is a *"zoonotic"* infection, which is a contagious disease that can be spread between both animals and humans.

This means that the organisms residing in the Leishmaniasis lesions can be communicated to humans.

Treatment in dogs is often difficult and the dog may suffer from relapses. Leishmaniasis poses a significant risk to the health of your dog, especially if you travel to the Mediterranean.

## c) Lyme Disease

This is one of the most common tick-borne diseases in the world, which is transmitted by Borrelia bacteria found in the deer or sheep tick.

Lyme disease, also called *"borreliosis"*, is also a zoonotic disease that can affect both humans and dogs and this disease can be fatal.

The Borrelia bacteria that causes Lyme's disease, is transmitted by slow-feeding, hard-shelled deer or sheep ticks, and the tick usually has to be attached to the dog for a minimum of 18 hours before the infection is transmitted.

Symptoms of this disease in a young or adult dog include:

- recurrent lameness from joint inflammation
- lack of appetite
- depression
- stiff walk with arched back
- sensitivity to touch
- swollen lymph nodes
- fever
- kidney damage
- rare heart or nervous system complications

While Lyme disease has been reported in dogs throughout the United States and Europe, it is most prevalent in the upper Mid-Western states, the Atlantic seaboard, and the Pacific coastal states.

In order to properly diagnose and treat Lyme disease, blood tests will be required, and if the tests are positive, oral antibiotics will be prescribed to treat the conditions.

Prevention is the key to keeping this disease under control because dogs that have had Lyme disease before are still able to get the disease again.

There is a vaccine for Lyme disease and dogs living in areas that have easy access to these ticks should be vaccinated yearly.

## d) Rocky Mountain Spotted Fever

This tick-transmitted disease is very often seen in dogs in the East, Midwest, and plains region of the US, and the organisms causing Rocky Mountain Spotted Fever (RMSF) are transmitted by both the American dog tick and the RMSF tick, which must be attached to the dog for a minimum of five hours in order to transmit the disease.

Common symptoms of RMSF include:

- fever
- reduced appetite
- depression
- pain in the joints
- lameness
- vomiting
- diarrhea

Some dogs affected with RMSF may develop heart abnormalities, pneumonia, kidney failure, liver damage, or even neurological signs, such as seizures or unsteady, wobbly or stumbling gait.

Diagnosis of this disease requires blood testing and if the results are positive, oral antibiotics will be given to the infected dog for approximately two weeks.

Dogs that can clear the organism from their systems will recover and after being infected, will remain immune to future infection.

## e) Ehrlichiosis

This is another tick borne disease transmitted by both the brown dog tick and the Lone Star Tick.

Ehrlichiosis has been reported in every state in the US, as well as worldwide. Common symptoms include:

- depression
- reduced appetite
- fever
- stiff and painful joints
- bruising

Signs of infection typically occur less than a month after a tick bite and last for approximately four weeks. There is no vaccine available.

Blood tests may be required to test for antibodies and treatment will require a course of antibiotics for up to four weeks in order to completely clear the organism from the infected dog's system.

After a dog has been previously infected, they may develop antibodies to the organism, but will not be immune to being re-infected.

Dogs living in areas of the country where the Ehrlichiosis tick diseases are common or widespread may be prescribed low doses of antibiotics during tick season.

**f) Anaplasmosis**

Deer ticks and western blacklegged ticks are carriers of the bacteria that transmit canine Anaplasmosis.

However, there is also another form of Anaplasmosis (caused by different bacteria) that is carried by the brown dog tick. Because the deer tick also carries other diseases, some animals may be at risk for developing more than one tick-borne disease at the same time.

Signs of Anaplasmosis are similar to Ehrlichiosis and include painful joints, diarrhea, fever, and vomiting as well as possible nervous system disorders.

 A dog will usually begin to show signs of Anaplasmosis within a couple of weeks after infection and diagnosis will require blood and urine testing, and sometimes other specialized laboratory tests.

Treatment is with oral antibiotics for up to 30 days, depending on how severe the infection may be.

When this disease is quickly treated, most dogs will recover completely, however, subsequent immunity is not guaranteed, which means that a dog may be re-infected if exposed again.

**g) Tick Paralysis**

Tick paralysis is caused when ticks secrete a toxin that affects the nervous system.

Affected dogs show signs of weakness and limpness approximately one week after being first bitten by ticks.

Symptoms usual begin with a change in pitch of the dog's usual bark, which will become softer, and weakness in the rear legs that eventually involves all four legs, which is then followed by the dog showing difficulty breathing and swallowing.

If the condition is not diagnosed and properly treated, death can occur.

Treatment involves locating and removing the tick and then treating the infected dog with tick anti-serum.

**h) Canine Coronavirus**

While this highly contagious intestinal disease, which is spread through the feces of contaminated dogs, was first discovered in

Germany during 1971 when there was an outbreak in sentry dogs, it is now found worldwide.

This virus can be destroyed by most commonly available disinfectants.

Symptoms include:

- diarrhea
- vomiting
- weight loss or anorexia

While deaths resulting from this disease are rare, and treatment generally requires only medication to relieve the diarrhea, dogs that are more severely affected may require intravenous fluids to combat dehydration.

There is a vaccine available, which is usually given to puppies, because they are more susceptible at a young age. This vaccine is also given to show dogs that have a higher risk of exposure to the disease.

## i) Leptospirosis

This is a disease that occurs throughout the World that can affect many different kinds of animals, including dogs, and as it is also a zoonotic disease, this means that it can affect humans, too. There is potential for both dogs and humans to die from this disease.

The disease is always present in the environment, which makes it easy for any dog to pick up. This is because it is found in many common animals, such as rats, and wildlife, as well as domestic livestock.

Veterinarians generally see more cases of Leptospirosis in the late summer and fall, which is probably because that is when more pets and wildlife are out and about.

More cases also occur after heavy rain falls.

155

The disease is most common in mild or tropical climates around the World, and in the US or Canada, it is more common in states or provinces that receive heavy rainfall.

The good news is that you can protect your dog from leptospirosis by vaccination, and while puppies are not routinely vaccinated against leptospirosis because chances of contracting the disease depends upon the lifestyle of the dog as well as the area in which the dog lives, it makes sense to vaccinate against this disease if you and your dog do live in an area considered a hot spot for leptospirosis, so ask your veterinarian.

City rat populations are a major carrier of leptospirosis.

Cold winter conditions lower the risk because the leptospira organisms do not tolerate the freezing and thawing of near-zero temperatures.

They are killed rapidly by drying, but they persist in standing water, dampness, mud and alkaline conditions.

Most of the infected wild animals and domestic animals that spread leptospirosis do not appear ill.

The leptospira take up residence in the kidneys of infected animals, which can include rats, mice, squirrels, skunks, and raccoons and when these animals void urine, they contaminate their environment with living leptospira.

Dogs usually become infected after sniffing urine or by wading, swimming or drinking contaminated water that has infected urine in it, and this is how the disease passes from animal to animal.

As well, the leptospira can also enter through a bite wound or if a dog eats infected material.

## 5) *Additional Vaccinations*

Depending upon where you and your Coton de Tulear live, your veterinarian may suggest additional vaccinations to help combat diseases that may be more common in your area.

## 6) *The Vaccinations Schedule*

The first vaccination needle is normally given to a puppy around six to eight weeks of age, which means that generally it will be the responsibility of the Coton de Tulear breeder to ensure that the puppy's first shots have been received before their new owner takes them home.

Thereafter, it will be the new Coton de Tulear puppy's guardians that will be responsible for ensuring that the next two sets of shots, which are usually given three to four weeks after each other, are given by the new guardian's veterinarian at the proper intervals.

## 7) *De-Worming the Dog*

De-worming kills internal parasites that your dog or puppy may have.

**NOTE**: no matter how sanitary your conditions, or where you live, your dog will have internal parasites, because it is not a matter of cleanliness.

It is recommended by the Center for Disease Control (CDC) that puppies be de-wormed every 2 weeks until they are 3 months old, and then every month after that, in order to control worms. Many veterinarians recommend worming dogs for tapeworm and roundworms every 6-12 months.

## *8) Poison Control*

### a. Knowing Poisonous Foods

While some dogs are smart enough not to want to eat foods that can harm or kill them, other canine companions will eat absolutely anything they can get their teeth on.

As conscientious guardians for our fur friends, it will always be our responsibility to make certain that when we share our homes with a dog, we never leave foods that could be toxic or lethal to them easily within their reach.

While there are many foods that can be toxic to a Coton de Tulear, the following alphabetical list contains some of the more common foods that can seriously harm or even kill our dogs including:

**Bread Dough**: if your dog eats bread dough, their body heat will cause the dough to rise inside the stomach. As the dough expands during the rising process, alcohol is produced.

Dogs who have eaten bread dough may experience stomach bloating, abdominal pain, vomiting, disorientation and depression. Because bread dough can rise to many times its original size, eating only a small amount will cause a problem for any dog.

**Broccoli**: the toxic ingredient in broccoli is isothiocynate. While it may cause stomach upset, it probably won't be very harmful unless the amount eaten is more than 10% of the dog's total daily diet.

**Chocolate**: contains theobromine, a chemical that is toxic to dogs in large enough quantities. Chocolate also contains caffeine, which is found in coffee, tea, and certain soft drinks. Different types of chocolate contain different amounts of theobromine and caffeine.

For example, dark chocolate and baking chocolate or cocoa powder contain more of these compounds than milk chocolate does, therefore, a dog would need to eat more milk chocolate in order to become ill.

However, even a few ounces of chocolate can be enough to cause illness or death in a puppy or smaller dog, like the Coton de Tulear, therefore, no amount or type of chocolate should be considered safe for a dog to eat.

Chocolate toxicity can cause vomiting, diarrhea, rapid or irregular heart rate, restlessness, muscle tremors, and seizures. Death can occur within 24 hours of eating.

During many holidays such as Christmas, New Year's, Valentine's, Easter and Halloween, chocolate is often more easily accessible to curious dogs, especially from children who are not so careful with where they might keep their Halloween or Easter egg stash and who are an easy mark for a hungry dog.

In some cases, people unwittingly poison their dogs by offering them chocolate as a treat or leaving chocolate cookies or frosted cake easily within licking distance.

**Caffeine**: beverages containing caffeine, such as soda, tea, coffee, and chocolate, act as a stimulant and can accelerate your dog's heartbeat to a dangerous level. Dogs eating caffeine have been known to have seizures, some of which are fatal.

**Cooked Bones**: can be extremely hazardous for a dog because the bones become brittle when cooked which causes them to splinter when the dog chews on them.

The splinters have sharp edges that have been known to become stuck in the teeth, and cause choking when caught in the throat or create a rupture or puncture of the stomach lining or intestinal tract.

Especially dangerous are cooked turkey and chicken legs, ham, pork chop and veal bones. Symptoms of choking include:

- Pale or blue gums
- Gasping open-mouthed breathing
- Pawing at the face
- Slow, shallow breathing
- Falling unconscious with dilated pupils

**Grapes and Raisins**: can cause acute (sudden) kidney failure in dogs. While it is not known what the toxic agent is in this fruit, clinical signs can occur within 24 hours of eating and include vomiting, diarrhea, and lethargy (tiredness).

Other signs of illness caused from eating grapes or raisins relate to the eventual shutdown of kidney functioning.

**Garlic and Onions**: contain chemicals that damage red blood cells by rupturing them so that they lose their ability to carry oxygen effectively, which leaves the dog short of oxygen, causing what is called *"hemolytic anemia"*.

Poisoning can occur with a single ingestion of large quantities of garlic or onions or with repeated meals containing small amounts.

Cooking does not reduce the potential toxicity of onions and garlic.

**NOTE**: fresh, cooked, and/or powdered garlic or onions are commonly found in baby food, which is sometimes given to dogs when they are sick, therefore, be certain to carefully read food labels before feeding to your Coton de Tulear.

**Macadamia Nuts**: are commonly found in candies and chocolates. Although the mechanism of macadamia nut toxicity is not well understood, the clinical signs in dogs having eaten these nuts include depression, weakness, vomiting, tremors, joint pain, and pale gums.

Signs can occur within 12 hours after eating. In some cases, symptoms can resolve themselves without treatment within 24 to 48 hours, however, keeping a close eye on your Coton de Tulear will be strongly recommended.

**Mushrooms**: mushroom poisoning can be fatal if certain species of mushrooms are eaten.

The most commonly reported severely toxic species of mushroom in the US is Amanita phalloides (Death Cap mushroom), which is also quite a common species found in most parts of Britain. Other Amanita species are also toxic.

This deadly mushroom is often found growing in grassy or wooded areas near various deciduous and coniferous trees, which mean that if you're out walking with your Coton de Tulear in the woods, they could easily find these mushrooms.

Eating them can cause severe liver disease and neurological disorders. If you suspect your dog has eaten these mushrooms, immediately take them to your veterinarian, as the recommended treatment is to induce vomiting and to give activated charcoal. Further treatment for liver disease may also be necessary.

**Pits and Seeds**: many seeds and pits found in a variety of fruits, including apples, apricots, cherries, pears and plums, contain cyanogenic glycosides that can cause cyanide poisoning in your Coton de Tulear.

The symptoms of cyanide poisoning usually occur within 15-20 minutes to a few hours after eating and symptoms can include initial excitement, followed by rapid respiration rate, salivation, voiding of urine and feces, vomiting, muscle spasm, staggering, and coma before death.

Dogs suffering from cyanide poisoning that live more than 2 hours after onset of symptoms will usually recover.

**Raw Salmon or Trout**: Salmon Poisoning Disease (SPD) can be a problem for anyone who goes fishing with their dog, or feeds their dog a raw meat diet that includes raw salmon or trout.

When a snail is infected and then is eaten by the fish, as part of the food chain, the dog is exposed when it eats the infected fish.

A sudden onset of symptoms can occur 5-7 days after eating the infected fish. In the acute stages, gastrointestinal symptoms are quite similar to canine parvovirus.

SPD has a mortality rate of up to 90%, can be diagnosed with a fecal sample and is treatable if caught in time.

Prevention is simple, cook all fish before feeding it to your Coton de Tulear and immediately see your veterinarian if you suspect that your dog has eaten raw salmon or trout.

**Tobacco**: all forms of tobacco, including patches, nicotine gum and chewing tobacco can be fatal to dogs if eaten.

Signs of poisoning can appear within an hour and include hyperactivity, salivation, panting, vomiting and diarrhea.

Advanced signs include muscle weakness, twitching, collapse, coma, increased heart rate and eventually cardiac arrest.

Never leave tobacco products within reach of your Coton de Tulear, and be careful not to let them pick up discarded cigarette butts when they are young puppies.

If you suspect your dog has eaten any of these, seek immediate veterinary help.

**TIP**: when your Coton de Tulear is a very young puppy, use a double leash, collar and harness arrangement, so that you can still teach them to walk on leash with a Martingale collar around their neck, but can also attach the second leash to their harness so that you can easily lift them over enticing cigarette butts or other toxic garbage they may be trying to eat during your walks.

**Tomatoes**: contain atropine, which can cause dilated pupils, tremors and irregular heartbeat. The highest concentration of atropine is found in the leaves and stems of tomato plants, next is the unripe (green) tomatoes, followed by the ripe tomato.

**Xylitol**: is an artificial sweetener found in products such as gum, candy, mints, toothpaste, and mouthwash that is recognized by the National Animal Poison Control Center to be a risk to dogs.

Xylitol is harmful to dogs because it causes a sudden release of insulin in the body that leads to hypoglycemia (low blood sugar). Xylitol can also cause liver damage in dogs.

Within 30 minutes after eating a product containing xylitol, the dog may vomit, be lethargic (tired), and/or be uncoordinated. However, some signs of toxicity can also be delayed for hours or even for a few days. Xylitol toxicity in dogs can be fatal if left untreated.

Please be aware that the above list is just some of the more common foods that can be toxic or fatal to our fur friends and that there are many other foods we should never be feeding our dogs.

If you have one of those dogs who will happily eat anything that looks or smells even slightly like food, be certain to keep these foods far away from your beloved Coton de Tulear and you'll help them to live a long and healthy life.

### b. Poisonous Plants Inside Your Home

Many common house plants are actually poisonous to our canine companions, and although many dogs simply will ignore house plants, some will attempt to eat anything, especially puppies who want to taste everything in their new world.

More than 700 plant species contain toxins that may harm or be fatal to puppies or dogs, depending on the size of the puppy or dog and how much they may eat. It will be especially important to be aware of household plants that could be toxic when you are sharing your home with a new puppy.

Following is a short list of the more common household plants, what they look like, the different names they are known by, and what symptoms would be apparent if your puppy or dog decides to eat them.

**Aloe Plant**: (medicine plant or Barbados aloe), is a very common succulent that is toxic to dogs. The toxic agent in this plant is Aloin.
This bitter yellow substance is found in most aloe species and may cause vomiting and/or reddish urine.

**Asparagus Fern**: (emerald feather, emerald fern, sprengeri fern, plumosa fern, lace fern). The toxic agent in this plant is sapogenin — a steroid found in a variety of plants. Berries of this plant cause vomiting, diarrhea and/or abdominal pain or skin inflammation from repeated exposure.

164

**Corn Plant**: (cornstalk plant, dracaena, dragon tree, ribbon plant) is toxic to dogs. Saponin is the offensive chemical compound found in this plant. If the plant is eaten, vomiting (with or without blood), loss of appetite, depression and/or increased salivation can occur.

**Cyclamen**: (Sowbread) is a pretty, flowering plant that, if eaten, can cause increased salivation, vomiting and diarrhea. If a dog eats a large amount of the plant's tubers, which are usually found below the soil at the root — heart rhythm abnormalities, seizures and even death can occur.

**Dieffenbachia**: (dumb cane, tropic snow, exotica) contains a chemical that is a poisonous deterrent to animals. If the plant is eaten, oral irritation can occur, especially on the tongue and lips. This irritation can lead to increased salivation, difficulty swallowing and vomiting.

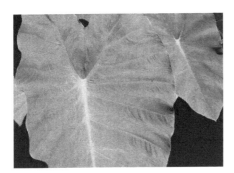

**Elephant Ear**: (caladium, taro, pai, ape, cape, via, via sori, malanga) contains a chemical similar to that found in dieffenbachia, therefore, a dog's toxic reaction to elephant ear is similar: oral irritation, increased salivation, difficulty swallowing and vomiting.

**Heartleaf Philodendron**: (horsehead philodendron, cordatum, fiddle leaf, panda plant, split-leaf philodendron, fruit salad plant, red emerald, red princess, saddle leaf), is a common, easy-to-grow houseplant that contains a chemical irritating to the mouth, tongue and lips of dogs. An affected dog may also experience increased salivation, vomiting and difficulty swallowing.

**Jade Plant**: (baby jade, dwarf rubber plant, jade tree, Chinese rubber plant, Japanese rubber plant, friendship tree). While the toxic property in this plant is unknown, eating it can cause depression, loss of coordination and, although more rare, slow heart rate.

**Lilies**: some plants of the lily family are toxic to dogs. The peace lily (also known as Mauna Loa) is toxic to dogs. Eating the peace lily or calla lily can cause irritation of the tongue and lips, increased salivation, difficulty swallowing and vomiting.

**Satin Pothos**: (silk pothos), if eaten by a dog, the plant may cause irritation to the mouth, lips and tongue, while the dog may also experience increased salivation, vomiting and/or difficulty swallowing.

The plants noted above are only a few of the more common household plants, and every conscientious Coton de Tulear guardian will want to educate themselves before bringing plants into the home that could be toxic to their canine companions.

## c. Poisonous Garden Plants

Please note that there are also many outdoor plants that can be toxic or poisonous to your Coton de Tulear, therefore, always check what plants are growing in your garden and if any may be harmful, remove them or make certain that your Coton de Tulear puppy or adult dog cannot eat them.

Cornell University, Department of Animal Science lists many different categories of poisonous plants affecting dogs, including house plants, flower garden plants, vegetable garden plants, plants found in swamps or moist areas, plants found in fields, trees and shrubs, plants found in wooded areas, and ornamental plants.

## d. Poison Proofing

You can learn about many potentially toxic and poisonous sources both inside and outside your home by visiting the ASPCA Animal Poison Control Center website.

Always keep your veterinarian's emergency number in a place where you can quickly access it, as well as the Emergency Poison Control telephone number, in case you suspect that your dog may have been poisoned.

Knowing what to do if you suspect your dog may have been poisoned and being able to quickly contact the right people could save your Coton de Tulear's life.

If you keep toxic cleaning substances (including fertilizers, vermin or snail poisons and vehicle products) in your home or garage, always keep them behind closed doors.

As well, keep any medications where your Coton de Tulear can never get to them, and seriously consider eliminating the use of any and all toxic products, for the health of both yourself and your best friend.

## e. Symptoms of Poisoning

It is impossible to keep guard over your pet at all times. Naturally, it opens a window of opportunity for your pet to explore around your place. And when it is on this mission, it seldom will respect the boundaries you set for your pet.

On its exploration spree, it can come into contact with or try to ingest those items that can cause poisoning.

Here are some of the symptoms you should look out for that point towards the possibility of poisoning. So even if you were not on guard, you can save your pet from an unfortunate fate by rushing it to the vet in time.

- Abdominal pain.
  Your dog will suddenly begin to whine a lot and when you try to touch its abdomen, you will feel it has become tender.
- Coma.
  Your canine friend will refuse to respond to your orders and will remain in a subconscious state for extended periods of time.
  At this time, you should absolutely take no time to get it to a veterinary doctor as this symbolizes an aggravated stage of poisoning.
- Convulsions.
  Poison can trigger convulsions in your pet.
  Rush it to the vet immediately if your pet begins to convulse all of a sudden.
- Diarrhea.
  Poisons will disrupt its digestive system. So if you see unexplained loose stools, rush to the poison control center or vet immediately.
  Admittedly, this is a much "lighter" version of poisoning. Nevertheless, untimely help can lead it to a horrific fate.

- Drooling.
  It is not much of a problem as most Coton de Tulear dogs are likely to drool. It is normal for quite a few.
  However, if you observe your Coton de Tulear dog has suddenly started drooling even though it did not do so before, consult a vet.
- Irregular heartbeat.
  Placing a hand on its chest will tell you if its heartbeats are normal or not.
  Like humans, the heartbeats are quite superficial. If you see your Coton de Tulear dog exhibiting some of the aforementioned characteristics, immediately roll it over and feel for its heartbeat.
  If it is irregular, you know what you need to do!
- Difficulty breathing.
  It will become evident to you when and if your pet is facing difficulty breathing. It will be making a conscious effort to keep breathing and will refuse to perform any strenuous activities.
  This will become even more evident if you observe it closely for a few minutes while it is lying on the floor.
- Fatigue.
  If your canine companion feels tired, it will automatically show on its face.
  Just keep a close eye on the signs it is giving off and those that are normal to it. Any deviation is almost always an indicator of trouble.
- Swollen limbs.
  Toxins in poisons can cause swelling in its limbs as well as in its internal organs. If it becomes apparent on its limbs, rush it to the emergency services immediately.
  You never know if internal swelling like that on its windpipe might become a major threat to its survival.
- Vomiting.
  Anything that is not tolerated well by its body is likely to be expelled in the form of vomit.
  However, this does not happen every time it tries to ingest

poison. If you are sure there is absolutely no other reason why your pet should begin vomiting all of a sudden, rush it to the vet immediately. A stitch in time saves nine!

If you observe any or all of these symptoms in your pet and you know that they are not normal for it, consult a veterinarian immediately.

If it is too difficult to seek out a veterinarian, look for the nearest poison control center for dogs. In such a situation, time is extremely sensitive to your pet's health. So don't procrastinate and don't take any chances.

Your pet deserves the best so make sure you don't let it down on this!

**f.  Animal Poison Control Centers**

The ASPCA Animal Poison Control Center is staffed 24 hours a day, 365 days a year and is a valuable resource for learning about what plants are toxic and possibly poisonous to your dog.

a) USA Poison Emergency
Call: 1 (888) 426-4435
When calling the Poison Emergency number, a $65. US (£39.42) consultation fee may be applied to your credit card.

b) UK Poison Emergency

Call: 0800-213-6680 - Pet Poison Helpline (payable service)

Call: 0300 1234 999 - RSPCA

www.aspca.org = ASPCA Poison Control.

## 9)  *Micro-chipping and Tattooing*

**Micro-Chipping**

A microchip implant is a tiny integrated circuit, approximately twice the size of a large grain of rice, enclosed in glass that is implanted under the skin of a dog (or other animal) with a syringe.

The chip uses passive Radio Frequency Identification (RFID) technology, and is also known as a PIT tag (Passive Integrated Transponder).

The microchip is usually implanted, without anesthetic, into the scruff of a dog's neck by a veterinarian or shelter.

The microchip has no internal power source, which means that they must be read by a scanner or *"interrogator"* which energizes the capacitor in the chip, which then sends radio signals back to the scanner so that the identifying number can be read.

Manufacturers of microchips often donate scanners to animal shelters and veterinarian clinics and hospitals.

While many communities are proposing making micro-chipping of all dogs mandatory, such as N. Ireland, and micro-chipping is a requirements for any dogs traveling to the state of Hawaii, many others are not especially pleased with this idea because they believe it's just more big business for little reward.

For instance, while approximately one quarter of European dogs have a microchip implant, the idea is definitely lacking in popularity in the United States, where only 5% of dogs are micro-chipped.

Even though micro-chipping is used by animal shelters, pounds, animal control officers, breeders and veterinarians, in order to help return a higher percentage of lost canines to their owners, some of the resistance to this idea can be explained by inherent problems with the ability of some organizations to correctly read the implants.

As an example, if the scanner is not tuned to the same frequency as the implanted microchip, it will not be read, which renders the process useless.

Pet microchips are manufactured with different frequencies, including 125 kHz, 128 kHz and 134.2 kHz.

While approximately 98% of the pet microchips in the US use 125 kHz, those in Europe use 134.2 kHz.

In other words, if the facility reading your dog's microchip does not have a compatible scanner, your dog will not be identified and returned to you.

Further, what may turn out to be worse than the scanner incompatibility problem could be increasing evidence to indicate that microchips can cause cancer.

As well some microchips will migrate inside the dog's body and while they may start out in the dog's neck, they could end up in their leg or some other body part.

You will have to weigh information known about microchips, including possible cancer risks, and the odds of losing your dog against whether or not a microchip is something you want to have for your Coton de Tulear.

Whether or not you choose a microchip for your dog, generally the cost ranges between $25 and $50 (£15 and £30) depending on what your veterinarian may charge for this service.

**Tattooing**

Dogs are tattooed to help identify them in case they are lost or stolen and many dog guardians prefer this safe, simple solution over micro-chipping.

Tattooing does not require locating a scanner that reads the correct frequency and there are no known side effects.

Because a tattoo is visible, it is immediately recognizable and reported when a lost dog is found, which means that tattooing could easily be the most effective means of identification available.

As well, dog thieves are less likely to steal a dog that has a permanent visible form of identification. There are several registries for tattooed dogs, including the National Dog Tattoo Registry in the UK, which has a network of Accredited Tattooists across the UK.

The fee for tattooing and registering a dog for their lifetime is approximately £25.

In the United States, the National Dog Registry (NDR) was founded in 1966 and since then, NDR has supervised, directed, conducted, or overseen the tattooing of more than 6 million animals.

The cost for tattooing a single dog is approximately $10 plus a one-time registration fee of $45.

## *10)  Licensing*

Many cities and jurisdictions around the world require that dogs be licensed.

Usually a dog license is an identifying tag that the dog will be required to wear on their collar. The tag will have an identifying number and a contact number for the registering organization, so that if someone finds a lost dog wearing a tag, the owner of the dog can be contacted.

Most dog tags are only valid for one year, and will need to be renewed annually at the beginning of every New Year, which involves paying a fee, which can vary from jurisdiction to jurisdiction.

From one extreme to the next, owners of dogs living in Beijing, China must pay a licensing fee of $600. (£360), while those living in Great Britain require no fee, because licensing of dogs was abolished in 1987.

Ireland and Northern Ireland both require dogs to be licensed and in Germany dog ownership is taxed, rather than requiring licensing, with higher taxes being paid for breeds of dogs deemed to be "dangerous".

Most US states and municipalities have licensing laws in effect and Canadian, Australian and New Zealand dogs also must be licensed, with the yearly fee approximately $30 to $50 (£18 to £30) depending upon whether the dog has been spayed or neutered.

## *11) Pet Insurance*

Pet guardians commonly ask themselves, when considering medical insurance for their dog, whether they can afford not to have it.

On the one hand, in light of all the new treatments and medications that are now available for our dogs which usually come with a very high price tag, an increasing number of guardians have decided to add pet insurance to their list of monthly expenses.

On the other hand, some humans believe that placing money into a savings account, in case unforeseen medical treatments are required, makes more sense.

Pet insurance coverage can cost anywhere from $2,000 to $6,000 USD (£1201 to £3604) over an average lifespan of a dog, and unless your dog is involved in a serious accident, or contracts a life-threatening disease, you may never need to pay out that much for treatment.

Whether you decide to start a savings account for your Coton de Tulear so that you will always have funds available for unforeseen health issues, or you decide to buy a health insurance plan, most dog lovers will go to any lengths to save the life of their beloved companions.

Having access to advanced technological tools and procedures means that our dogs are now being offered treatment options that were once only reserved for humans.

Now, some canine conditions that were once considered fatal, are being treated at considerable costs ranging anywhere between $1,000 and $5,000 (£597 and £2,986) and more.

However, even in the face of rapidly increasing costs of caring for our dogs, owners purchasing pet insurance remain a small minority.

In an effort to increase the numbers of people buying pet insurance, insurers have teamed with the American Kennel Club and Petco Animal Supplies to offer the insurance, and more than 1,600 companies, such as Office Depot and Google, offer pet insurance coverage to their employees as an optional employee benefit.

Even though you might believe that pet insurance will be your savior anytime your dog needs a trip to the vet's office, you really need to be careful when considering an insurance plan, because there are many policies that contain small print excluding certain ages, hereditary or chronic conditions.

Unfortunately, most people don't consider pet insurance when their pets are healthy because buying pet insurance means playing the odds, and unless your dog becomes seriously ill, you end up paying for something that may never happen.

However, just like automobile insurance, you can't buy it after you've had that accident. Therefore, since many of us, in today's uncertain economy, may be hard pressed to pay a high veterinarian bill, generally speaking, the alternative of paying monthly pet insurance premiums will provide peace of mind and improved veterinarian care for our best friends.

Shop around, because as with all insurance policies, pet insurance policies will vary greatly between companies and the only way to know for certain exactly what sort of coverage you are buying is to be holding a copy of that policy in your hand so that you can clearly read what will and what will not be covered. Don't forget to carefully read the fine print to avoid any nasty surprises, because the time to discover that a certain procedure will not be covered is not when you are in the middle of filing a claim.

**Before Purchasing a Policy**

- There are several considerations to be aware of before choosing to purchase a pet insurance policy, including: Is your dog required to undergo a physical exam?
- Is there a waiting period before the policy becomes active?
- What percentage of the bill does the insurance company pay — after the deductible?
- Are payments limited or capped in any way?
- Are there co-pays (cost to you up front)?
- Does the plan cover pre-existing conditions?
- Does the plan cover chronic or recurring medical problems?
- Can you choose any vet or animal hospital to treat your pet?
- Are prescription medications covered?
- Are you covered when traveling with your pet?
- Does the policy pay if your pet is being treated and then dies?

When you love your dog and worry that you may not have the funds to cover an emergency medical situation that could unexpectedly cost thousands, the right pet insurance policy will provide both peace of mind and better health care for your beloved fur friend.

# Chapter 14: Financial Aspects

The Coton de Tulear dog is a fairly expensive breed – from all aspects. Their acquisition costs are quite high, ranging between several thousands. At the same time, their constant upkeep and maintenance also incurs additional costs. If you are looking for a realistic estimate, here it is!

Prior owners of Coton de Tulear dogs observe that their pet consumes, on the average, about $2,500 from their yearly budget! This estimate is a moderate one that you need to spend on your Coton de Tulear dog's upkeep. If you try to be a "giving" master, you can expect these figures to sky-rocket to colossal heights!

## 1) Food

The primary and most repetitive cost in this figure is the cost of its food – an expense that you need to make in all cases. Coton de Tulear dogs need high quality dry dog food. If you try to put them on people food, they are likely to develop health problems which will end up costing you significantly more than the amount you saved on dog food!

The best ones in the market cost between $25 and $30 per month. This means you would incur roughly $300 per year. Since the Coton de Tulear dog is comparatively of a small size, it wouldn't consume a lot. Therefore these costs will not be much substantial.

Moreover, you might want to include the cost of treats and other supplements that you decide to give to your pet. The treats alone can incur an additional cost up to $20 for a bag. Vitamins and other supplements may have varying costs depending on their composition ranging between $10 and $250 per bottle. Generally, you do not need to worry about vitamins and supplements if you have a puppy. The same, however, cannot be said for the aged Coton de Tulear dogs.

When it is about taking care of your pet, the sky is the only limit about what it may cost you!

## 2) *Accessories*

The estimate mentioned above does not include the cost of dog accessories like the travel crate, dog toys and other items of use. Usually these are purchased well in advance and can be used for years at a stretch.

If you are still looking for an estimate, consider this; an average travel crate for your Coton de Tulear can cost between $80 and $100! As the Coton de Tulear does not grow much in size, making intelligent choices can save you quite a few bucks in the long run.

As far as its grooming is concerned, be ready to spend another couple of hundreds on these accessories. For instance, you can get nail clippers and trimmers for $20 to $60. A regular hair brush can cost you about $15; an organic one would be slightly more expensive. Pet wipes may cost about $20 per pack and medicated shampoos can cost you about the same. If you purchase them all, you may incur a cost of $100 to $150 or more on grooming supplies alone.

If you are taking your Coton de Tulear in for some professional grooming, be ready to spend anywhere between $30 and $50 per visit. Seeing the quality and length of hair that a Coton de Tulear has, it is encouraged for you to take your pet over for professional grooming services at some point or the other.

Collars and leashes are another important expense that can cost you anything between $10 (for the most basic accessory) to $70 (for more stylish equipment with multiple utility). If you decide to add in a couple of flashy identification tags to the collar, you can add in a few more bucks to compensate for that. The purpose served by the $10 leash will be more or less the same as that of the $70 one. The only difference is that the latter might offer you options to "fasten" your pet into your car as well.

Dog toys are relatively inexpensive. You can get a bunch of these for $10 and they would be durable enough to last six months if not one year! If you go for stuffed toys, the cost may be slightly higher – about $15 for a toy. Nevertheless, these costs are very well justified and contribute a small portion of your overall expenses.

## 3) The Vet

Your concerns don't end here. There is the annual trip to the veterinary doctor as well that is bound to gouge a significant hole in your financial resources.

It largely depends on the locality you live in. In some place, you can find veterinary services for much cheaper than in other places. On the whole, it can cost you about $250 to $1,000. If you are looking for specialized services like micro chipping, the costs will be significant and charged separately. Any other surgical procedures that your pet needs will incur costs over the given estimate.

The annual checkup costs tend to be larger for two reasons – firstly, you are not making a payment out of your pockets every month; secondly, this cost generally includes the expenses pertaining to blood tests, heartworm tests and several other similar examinations. The cost of yearly vaccinations is also embedded in this cost. Hence the mountainous amount is justified.

Alternatively, if you go for semi-annual checkups, it will cost you about $100 to $150 per visit. The scarcity of such services has contributed towards selective inflation in this segment of medical care. Make sure you check in with your preferred veterinarian beforehand to get a realistic estimate of your yearly budget.

If you settle for a diseased puppy or a disease-prone breed, rest assured your medical care costs will be significantly higher than those mentioned in here. This is also one of the reasons why purchasing registered dogs from authentic breeders is encouraged.

Additionally, the cost of spaying or neutering a Coton de Tulear dog is also quite high. If you want to get a female Coton de Tulear spayed, it will cost you between $170 and $240. The cost of neutering male Coton de Tulear dogs range between $120 and $175. This is a onetime expenditure and hence should not be a major concern for you. You can also find non-profit charitable organizations in your vicinity to help take care of your pet if the costs are getting too high beyond affordability.

## 4) Dog Training

And this brings us to another most important financial aspect to owning a Coton de Tulear dog – the cost of training. This also depends on your locality and if you are lucky you might be able to find certain resources that are more affordable.

On average, a single training class with the training center can cost you between $15 and $45. Group classes average for $150 to $250 for a four to six week schedule respectively. The twist here is this; there are more than a dozen training courses for dogs! Each training course comes at a price. So if you add it all up, you will end up with a figure that may be out of reach.

For this reason, conducting a needs assessment beforehand will be a good option. As an owner, you have the right kind of experience to understand what kind of training your pet needs. Consequently, you can work in collaboration with your local training centers to work on those areas that demand attention. Getting your pet to behave well is definitely a priority as compared with having your pet fetch various things on your order.

If you are unclear about what type of training classes your pet needs in order to improve its responses, you can consult and discuss it with training experts available at the center. They will guide you through the process in the best possible manner while making sure the results you seek are delivered.

## 5) *Miscellaneous Expenses*

There are a few other dog accessories – like the dog gates, barriers and other similar installations – for which an estimate has not been included deliberately. It all depends on you – how much you are willing to spend. The more you spend, the more accessories your pet will have. Even though this does not always translate into its happiness, it does mean exaggerated comfort for your beloved canine friend.

Apart from all these costs, you should be prepared for property damage as well when and if the Coton de Tulear dog becomes too agitated to calm down. It can wreck havoc in your living space, tear up the sofas and curtains and is very well equipped to slip through your doors too! Usually training does the trick but it pays to be safe and anticipate the worst even if it isn't happening!

Usually the first year is the hardest and the most expensive. This is the time when your pet is settling in and is therefore going through a number of adjustment issues. So when and if it tries to express its anger or frustration, it can end up costing you a couple of dollars. However, over time, your pet will learn to respect your authority and will therefore make things much easier.

All the figures given in here are estimates. Actual prices of commodities may vary. A range has been given to accommodate the expensive as well as inexpensive options.

In fact, the yearly estimates given above also pertain to situations where you keep away from unnecessary and luxurious expenditures. The more you try to pamper your pet, the higher the total costs will become! Even though your pet does not really understand "money" as much as it understands "love", it will nevertheless like being pampered. For Coton de Tulear dogs, their luxury threshold is reached sooner than most other breeds.

Keeping and maintaining a Coton de Tulear dog is by no means an easy feat. It does not only demand a significant portion of your finances but also an equally exhaustive slice of your time and effort. There is a lot you need to do to make this association work out positively. Although the Coton de Tulear dog is an intelligent learner, it nevertheless will not be able to understand your rules if you do not make a conscious effort to get the right message across.

So do you really have it in you to own a Coton de Tulear dog and also provide nothing but the best for it?!

# Chapter 15: General Tips, Tricks and Guidelines

Here are a few guidelines for taking care of a canine companion in general. Regardless of the breed that you own, you can care for your canine companion in a better way by keeping in mind the following things.

## *1) Helping the Puppy Transition*

The impending loss of a beloved dog is one of the most painfully difficult and emotionally devastating experiences a canine guardian will ever have to face.

For the sake of our faithful companions, because we do not want to prolong their suffering, we humans will have to do our best to look at our dog's situation practically, rather than emotionally, so that we can make the best decision for them.

They may be suffering from extreme old age and the inability to even walk outside to relieve themselves, and thus having to deal with the indignity of regularly soiling their sleeping area, they may have been diagnosed with an incurable illness that is causing them much pain, or they may have been seriously injured.

Whatever the reason for a canine's suffering, it will be up to their human guardian to calmly guide the end-of-life experience so that any further discomfort and distress can be minimized.

**What to Do If You Are Uncertain?**

In circumstances where it is not entirely clear how much a dog is suffering, it will be helpful to pay close attention to your Coton de Tulear dog's behavior and keep a daily log or record so that you can know for certain how much of their day is difficult and painful for them, and how much is not.

When you keep a daily log, it will be easier to decide if the dog's quality of life has become so poor that it makes better sense to offer them the gift of peacefully going to sleep.

During this time of uncertainty, it will also be very important to discuss with your veterinarian what signs of suffering may be associated with the dog's particular disease or condition, so that you know what to look for.

Often a dog may still continue to eat or drink despite being upset, having difficulty breathing, excessively panting, being disoriented or in much pain, and as their caring guardians, we will have to weigh their love of eating against how much they are really suffering in all other aspects of their life.

Obviously, if a canine guardian can clearly see that their beloved companion is suffering throughout their days and nights, it will make sense to help humanely end their suffering by planning a euthanasia procedure.

We humans are often tempted to delay the inevitable moment of euthanasia, because we love our dogs so much and cannot bear the anticipation of the intense grief we know will overwhelm us when we must say our final goodbyes to our beloved fur friend.

Unfortunately, we may regret that we allowed our dog to suffer too long, and could find ourselves wishing that if only we humans had the same option, to peacefully let go, when we find ourselves in such a stage in our own lives.

## 2) *Euthanasia – What, Why and How?*

Every veterinarian will have received special training to help provide all incurably ill, injured or aged pets that have come to the end of their natural lives with a humane and gentle death, through a process called *"euthanasia"*.

When the time comes, euthanasia, or putting a dog *"to sleep"*, will usually be a two-step process.

First, the veterinarian will inject the dog with a sedative to make them sleepy, calm and comfortable.

Second, the veterinarian will inject a special drug that will peacefully stop their heart.

These drugs work in such a way that the dog will not experience any awareness whatsoever that their life is ending. What they will experience is very much like what we humans experience when falling asleep under anesthesia during a surgical procedure.

Once the second stage drug has been injected, the entire process takes about 10 to 20 seconds, at which time the veterinarian will then check to make certain that the dog's heart has stopped.

There is no suffering with this process, which is a very gentle and humane way to end a dog's suffering and allow them to peacefully pass on.

## 3) Where Most Dog/Puppy Owners Go Wrong

Here are some of the common mistakes made by people while petting their canine companions.

Make sure you are not one of them as this can seriously disrupt your relationship with your Coton de Tulear dog at some point in time or the other!

### a. Experimentation

First and foremost, you should not experiment with your pet, especially in matters pertaining to its health.

Self-medication is the last thing you should do even if your pet seems to have developed a problem that had occurred previously. You might be inclined to do so in order to save some costs but do keep in mind the dog doesn't respond to medication in the same way as humans.

If and when your plan backfires, the results will be even more drastic!

**b. Sleeping in Your Bed**

As stressed on multiple occasions, you should never let the canine sleep with you in your bed. Many of us humans make the mistake of allowing a crying puppy to sleep in their bed, and while this may help to calm and comfort a new puppy, it will set a dangerous precedent that can result in behavioral problems later in their life.

As much as it may pull on your heart strings to hear your new Coton de Tulear puppy crying the first couple of nights in their kennel, a little tough love at the beginning will keep them safe while helping them to learn to both love and respect you as their leader.

**c. Playing Too Hard or Too Long**

Many humans play too hard or allow their children to play too long or too roughly with a young puppy.

You need to remember that a young puppy tires very easily and especially during the critical growing phases of their young life, they need their rest.

**d. Hand Play**

Always discourage your Coton de Tulear puppy from chewing or biting your hands, or any part of your body for that matter.

If you allow them to do this when they are puppies, they will want to continue to do so when they have strong jaws and adult teeth and this is not acceptable behavior for any breed of dog.

Do not get into the habit of playing the "hand" game, where you rough up the puppy and slide them across the floor with your hands, because this will teach your puppy that your hands are playthings.

When your puppy is teething, they will naturally want to chew on everything within reach, and this will include you. As cute as you might think it is, this is not an acceptable behavior and you need to gently, but firmly, discourage the habit.

A light flick with a finger on the end of a puppy nose, combined with a firm "NO" when they are trying to bite human fingers will discourage them from this activity.

### e. Extraordinary Creation

You should not consider it as an extraordinary being of any sort. It cannot take care of itself, cannot recognize what may be lethal for it and definitely cannot be expected to adapt or adjust to different settings.

It is not human, and you being its owner are responsible for keeping it healthy. Don't be negligent about your pet's needs – you never know when you might end up harming your own pal.

### f. Being Too Distracted

If you have too many distractions to keep you busy through days or nights, are planning to have a child of your own, are one of the laid back types or simply cannot devote time and attention to your pet for whatever reason, it is best to stay away from such a commitment.

Coton de Tulear dogs demand more effort as compared to other breeds. If you cannot keep up with its pace, well then don't get involved!

**g.  No Need for Training**

Besides this, never be misled into believing your Coton de Tulear dog is naturally well-behaved or does not need training because it seems to be doing very well without it.

Coton de Tulear dogs learn quickly and will therefore follow your orders easily. However, it wouldn't be long before its internal state of crisis will get into the way of obedience.

Start training the Coton de Tulear dog as early as possible to make sure that unfortunate occurrences can be kept to a bare minimum.

The more you delay training for your Coton de Tulear dog, the more stubborn and irresponsive it will become. So it is in your best interest not to procrastinate this duty.

**h.  Inconsistent Orders**

On the same note, make sure you (and your family) use consistent words for specific actions.

Your Coton de Tulear is not a human and will therefore become extremely confused if you use the same word and expect it to act differently.

Even if it is impulsively and linguistically right, the same cannot be said for your pet's understanding.

Consider this for example; if you want it to sit on the floor, you say "down" and when your spouse wants it off the sofa, they say "down". It will become worse when your kid says "down" to get the Coton de Tulear dog down a flight of stairs.

Linguistically, the word is used correctly in all three situations. But it is creating confusion in the mind of the Coton de Tulear about what the owner(s) wants.

It is best to use separate words for different actions and then reinforce this definition to make sure your Coton de Tulear dog respond well.

### i.   Not Using Enough Treats

It is recommended to use treats often, especially during the training phase. It is easily the best way to reinforce actions and responses.

So whenever your pet follows your orders or responds to the most recent training class, treat it with some snacks. It will know when it is being praised and will therefore respond to make you happy.

### j.   Leaving It off the Leash

Never try to leave your Coton de Tulear dog off the leash until and unless you are absolutely sure it is well disciplined.

Although it is encouraged to conduct your training sessions in public areas or in places where numerous distractions exist, make sure you do so once your pet has understood the basics.

Training amidst distractions makes sure your pet responds to your orders in similar situations.

But if you leave it off the leash before training sessions take effect, it is more likely to wander off to restricted territories, bite a few people or animals and get you into a lot of trouble that could have been avoided if you kept the leash intact!

### k.   Leaving it Unattended

Lastly and most importantly, don't let your pet get lonely or leave it unsupervised for long time periods.

It is a disastrous combination which can result in all sorts of damage – to your property as well as your pet. A lonely Coton de Tulear is likely to experiment with different objects within the house. Such activities are not always uneventful.

Also, don't leave it unsupervised in a place where known threats exist. For instance, don't keep it locked in the car or leave it around a park without supervision. Such negligence may end up inflicting irreversible pain to your pet.

**l.   Expecting too much!**

Don't expect too much from your pet in too little time. Patience and perseverance is the key to success. Let your Coton de Tulear dog settle in and absorb your rules – it will eventually get there. Haste can only make matters worse for you as well as for your newfound pet!

## *4)  Caring for Aged Dogs*

Caring for an aging dog is slightly different from caring for a puppy. Their demands and needs are infinitely different. It is common to come across one if you are involved in rescuing the Coton de Tulear breed. Here are some of the things you need to keep in mind while handling aged Coton de Tulear dogs.

Aged Coton de Tulear dogs, especially if they come from battered homes, are likely to have several health issues. Make sure you keep these in mind while preparing their meals and activities.

It is advised not to serve them any hard foods or bones that can damage their gums. Also, keep the oil content in foods low so that digestive issues can be kept to a minimum.

On this note, keep in mind that some of the health problems faced by your Coton de Tulear dog are likely to come naturally with age. There is no way to delay or eliminate these.

For instance, most aged dogs will experience reduced hearing and sight. Learn to differentiate between imminent dangers and the natural course of life.

Your veterinary doctor is more skilled to tell you about the different signs likely to be exhibited by your pet. However, it pays to consider anything out of the ordinary as a potential threat for your pet's well-being!

Aged Coton de Tulear dogs are not likely to be as energetic as young ones. Plan their activities in a placid manner.

Remember to take them out for walks and other activities as it helps prevent the arthritis from becoming a major problem.

Select a peaceful space in your house where they can rest through the day. You can take them for rides but beware of their stress urinary incontinence.

Don't forget the annual checkups. Better still increase its frequency to semi-annually.

As far as the vaccinations are concerned, ask your veterinary doctor if it is advisable to tune down the frequency to once every three years.

Besides this, you might need to use some vitamins and supplements to counter failing health. The rest all should be fine.

## 5) *Tackling the Natural Demise*

Some humans do not fully recognize the terrible grief involved in losing a beloved canine friend.

There will be many who do not understand the close bond we humans can have with our dogs, which is often unlike any we have with our human counterparts.

Your friends may give you pitying looks and try to cheer you up, but if they have never experienced such a loss themselves, they may also secretly think that you are making too much fuss over "just a dog".

For some of us humans, the loss of a beloved dog is so painful that we decide never to share our lives with another, because we cannot bear the thought of going through the pain of loss again.

Expect to feel terribly sad, tearful and yes, depressed because those who are close to their canine companions will feel their loss no less acutely than the loss of a human friend or life partner.

The grieving process can take some time to recover from, and some of us never totally recover.

After the loss of a family dog, first you need to take care of yourself by making certain that you keep eating and getting regular sleep, even though you will feel an almost eerie sense of loneliness.

Losing a beloved dog is a shock to the system, which can also affect your concentration and your ability to find joy or want to participate in other activities that may be part of your daily life.

During this early grieving time you will need to take extra care while driving or performing tasks that require your concentration as you may find yourself distracted.

If there are other dogs or pets in the home, they will also be grieving the loss of a companion, and may display this by acting depressed, being off their food or showing little interest in play or games. Therefore, you need to help guide your other pets through this grieving process by keeping them busy and interested, taking them for extra walks and spending more time with them.

Many people do not wait long enough before attempting to replace a lost pet and will immediately go to the local shelter and rescue a deserving dog.

While this may help to distract you from your grieving process, this is not really fair to the new fur member of your family.

Bringing a new pet into a home that is depressed and grieving the loss of a long time canine member may create behavioral problems for the new dog that will be faced with learning all about their new home while also dealing with the unstable, sad energy of the grieving family.

A better scenario would be to allow yourself the time to properly grieve by waiting a minimum of one month to allow yourself and your family to feel happier and more stable before deciding upon sharing your home with another dog.

The grieving process will be different for everyone and you will know when the time is right to consider sharing your home with another canine companion.

# Conclusion

The Coton de Tulear is an endearing dog breed. Much like any other dog breed, the Coton has its benefits and disadvantages. It is important for you to research well about this breed and analyze your lifestyle critically in order to lay the foundation of a promising relationship.

In many ways, the Coton can adapt to your lifestyle choices. In some places, you will need to make some compromises in order to allow the Coton to adjust. It is definitely a must-have dog breed if you are willing to make a few minor compromises with your lifestyle.

What makes it even more endearing is its sprightly nature, the ability to perform simple tricks to amuse onlookers and its affectionate personality! It is a crowd pleaser and can mingle with strangers quite easily.

It is an intelligent breed that will continue to surprise you. Although the Coton de Tulear is not very well adapted for guardian roles, it nevertheless serves as a trustworthy companion to have by your side.

On the whole it is considered to be an amiable dog – with friends as well as foes. It is therefore considered as one of the best dog breeds for you.

We wish you a pleasant companionship ahead!

# Published by IMB Publishing 2014

12772559R00113

Printed in Poland
by Amazon Fulfillment
Poland Sp. z o.o., Wrocław